God Isn't

Finished With

Me Yet!

By Kathy Hughes, with Rita Milios

Sow The Seed Ministries

First Printing 1990

Second Printing 1999 by Hardbound, Inc.,
St. Louis, Mo. 63031

Third Printing 2002 by Hardbound, Inc.,
St. Louis, Mo. 63031

Fourth Printing 2008 by Sow The Seed Ministries,
Glasgow KY 42141

Library of Congress Catalog Card No: 88-51484
ISBN: 1-55523-206-X

Printed in the United States of America

Dedication

My Support Group,
My Prayer Group,
My Genuine Friends who help me get
my life in order,
My family, especially my son Jonathan &
my Mother, my Saving Grace...

Special Note from Jonathan

When I was asked to write a special note for my mother's book, I looked at the task as if it were both a duty and a privilege. As I read her book, I realized that in my 19 years of knowing my mother I had never taken the time to learn about what are, for me, some of the most unfathomable events that have surely molded my mother into the irreplaceable person that she is today. Like many others who have read this work, I wanted to know who my mother is. But for me, digesting the words on these pages meant connecting with a big part of my own heritage, as well as trying to get a glimpse of who my mother was before her head injury. I was quick to ponder what her life might have been if this traumatic accident had never happened. But I also understand that thoughts like this are not in the spirit of my Mother's story.

To me, "God Isn't Finished With Me Yet" is about taking life's twists and turns and allowing these events to push us towards becoming better people. This story proves that with enough courage, determination and heart, we can make the impossible possible and hopefully wake from our dreams to find that they are our reality.

With all that said and done, I proudly present to you, the reader, "God Isn't Finished With Me Yet!" I truly hope you get as much out of it as I have.

Jonathan

TABLE OF CONTENTS

Foreword

In 1979, Kathy Hughes was a college graduate, establishing her career in social work. She was busy and active. Kathy was having fun, enjoying life, and looking forward to a bright future.

But on August 3, 1979, Kathy's life changed forever. She was in an automobile accident. She was thrown from the car, and her head smashed into the curb. The left side of her brain, the side responsible for language functions, was damaged beyond repair.

From that moment on, Kathy was a different person. She had aphasia. She could not speak, read, or write. For the next seven years, Kathy would fight a battle that seemed impossible to win.

But Kathy refused to accept that she might never communicate again with those around her. Although she was given little reason for hope, Kathy set out to prove that she could beat the odds. She would be "normal" again. Through years of hard work and in spite of several physical and emotional traumas along the way, Kathy never gave up. She fought her way back from a world of silence to regain both her ability to communicate and her independence. Kathy's story is one of courage and hope of what the human spirit can do when it is motivated by faith.

When I first met Kathy, seven years after her accident, we were strangers. She was a person with a story to tell, and she needed help telling it. I was a writer looking for work. We liked each other instantly. We felt a bond. Our meeting was meant to be.

So it was. Our lives became intertwined. We started out as boss and employee; we ended up as friends. Together we worked through Kathy's pain, shared her memories, and gave words to her feelings.

Often I felt like a Peeping Tom, peeking into the private corners of Kathy's mind. Kathy, who was such a private person, sometimes resisted giving the more intimate details that would make her story come alive. But she did it, because to Kathy, anything, even giving up her privacy, was worth the price if it helped her to achieve her goal.

Kathy's goal-to have her story told, to be understood, to help others-was the most important thing in her life. Rarely have I seen the determination, the single-minded dedication that I saw in Kathy. She knew, beyond the shadow of a doubt, that her book would be published, that it would help the families of others like her. Her struggle is indeed an inspiration. Kathy's faith is part of the legacy she brought with her from the accident. Once you have been as close to God as Kathy was, you become more aware of the mysterious forces that rule all our lives.

Kathy is indeed a special person. I did not know her before the accident, but her friends tell me she has changed. She is more focused and more productive in her life. Some say Kathy has lost some of her intellectual capacity. She was a promising college graduate one minute, and the next she could not speak. Yes, her brain was damaged. She does not have the range of speech that I do. She cannot describe in flowery language how she feels. But never, not once, have I doubted Kathy's intelligence. I never felt the need to talk down to Kathy, to slow my speech, or to change my vocabulary. We talked like two friends, with Kathy sometimes outtalking me. And even when I had to help her put words to her feelings, I could sense from Kathy what she was trying to say. It was there in a look, a sigh, or a tear in her eye. Kathy's ability to communicate is limited, but her mind is not.

It is true, however, that Kathy is not your ordinary brain trauma victim. The factors that make Kathy "Kathy" are the very things that helped her to achieve a level of recovery that many patients may never reach: her determination, her single-minded focus on her goals-to talk, to read, to write, to communicate again-and her willingness to do whatever it took to reach those goals. Others can do what Kathy did, if they try hard enough, if they want it enough to do whatever it takes. Kathy suffered through seven years of pain and isolation because she was willing to pay the price.

Now Kathy is reaping the rewards of a job well done. Congratulations, Kathy! And best of luck. You are a special person, an inspiration, a beacon of love and faith, shining brightly, lighting the darkness of despair with hope. God bless you!

Rita Milios

Preface

This is a book of Joy and Hope and Love

When one is facing an inability to communicate, which is the very essence of humanness, it may mean despair. One may evince terror. It is not a nightmare; it is real. This book is a bright spot in a world where the afflicted person is often overwhelmed by fear and hopelessness.

Kathy may have been a rebel, however she has evolved into a rebel with a cause: to develop a head trauma support group called *People Helping People*. She cajoles, encourages and loves those with serious problems and their accompanying physical deficits.

Her enthusiasm is contagious, her energy awesome and the joy that is a shining aura around her is beautiful to see. She may be unaware of her Love Power, but it is a part of her.

Kathy lived through a life-threatening head injury. She was helped immeasurably by quick and competent medical assistance. There were prayers for the surgeon and prayers for Kathy. She was surrounded by the love of her family and friends. But the turning point may have been when Kathy felt she heard a command from The Supreme Being: "Kathy, go back. I'm not finished with you yet."

There followed therapy with its constant, grueling, painful hours to cope with, but Kathy was sustained by the vision. She had been to the brink. She knew how beautiful the experience of dying is. She knew that a New Self was emerging from that encounter-a Self determined to recover, to realize the dream of helping make others whole and to help them with joy and serenity. Kathy is all this. She has a mission in life. She brings laughter and happy feelings to everyone whose life she touches. Her talks are down-to earth, full of insights and wit. When reading her book, one continually wonders what the next Chapter holds.

Kathy, through the experience of her book, brings

understanding to the uninitiated, comfort to the wounded and help to the caregivers. One is amazed at the candid glimpse into Kathy's feelings. Her techniques for coping should be lessons for us all.

Helen Harlan Wulf

Chapter 1

THE ACCIDENT

Jean Hughes smiled as she glanced sideways at her sister, Kathy, still staring dreamily out the car window. Kathy's thick, dark hair was held back by two tortoise shell combs; otherwise, it would have been impossible for Jean to see her sister's face. Jean often kidded Kathy, saying that both Kathy and her hair were untameable.

Kathy had always been a free spirit, unencumbered by many responsibilities or material needs. She relied more on fate than ambition to move her through life. Fun loving and adventuresome, Kathy ended up here in Port Clinton because she fell in love first with the tiny lakeside town, then with one of its residents. With a degree in sociology, and her natural friendliness, Kathy had easily landed a job at a nearby resort. Her relationship with Bill, a longtime Port Clinton resident, flourished, and Kathy finally took a social work job in 1973. Now, six years later, at the age of thirty, Kathy said she was ready to settle down. Jean marveled at how easily Kathy could switch gears and adapt to the changes in her life.

Kathy felt Jean's gaze and turned to meet her sister's eyes, large and gray like her own, but somewhat more subdued and introspective.

"Isn't it beautiful?" Kathy's tone demanded agreement. "I never get tired of looking at the sunset over Lake Erie."

"I admit the sunsets in St. Louis pale a little in comparison," laughed Jean. She took her eyes off the road in front of her long enough to look through the window on the passenger's side of the car. The sun hung low on the horizon, a blood red fireball against a gold and orange backdrop. The shoreline was already in shadows; jagged rocks stood out like broken teeth in the open mouth of the

11

lake.

Jean thought about the past week in Port Clinton with Kathy and all that she had learned about her sister. They had seldom been as close as they were right now. Growing up with ten other brothers and sisters around, they rarely found themselves alone. In these few days they had probably spent more time talking together than they had in all those years of living under the same roof. *I'm glad I came,* thought Jean.

As they reminisced, the sisters forged a bond between them consisting of more than memories. Jean saw some of her sister's independent nature in herself and she liked it, although she doubted that she would ever upstage her older sister as the rebel of the family.

"Remember the time you went to New Orleans for a friend's wedding and liked it so much you stayed for two years?" Jean had chided her. "And the time you volunteered to work with the migrant families in Texas? You always did live just one day at a time," she said.

As she recalled the recent nights when they had talked until dawn, Jean was reluctant to end her trip. *But all good things must come to an end,* she mused, *even Kathy's fun-loving flings.*

Jean noticed the long shadows quickly creeping over the landscape.

"Well, it's too late to go to the beach. The sun will be gone soon. What do you want to do now, Kathy?"

Kathy thought for a moment. "Oh, I don't know. Why don't we see if we can find Bill?"

Kathy just was not happy if she was away from Bill too long. She liked to know where he was at all times. "Let's try Phyl's Bar," she said.

Bill was a construction worker and spent many of his off hours relaxing with friends at a local tavern. He could usually be found there after work, playing pool and drinking beer. Kathy always liked to join him but for the past few weeks she had done little drinking.

Phyl's Bar was just a short distance away, but for Kathy

it may as well have been a lifetime. Much later she would remember little of what happened in the next few seconds; even then it would be like seeing it through a haze, smoky and far removed from reality. For Kathy, this brief moment in time created a new reality. It altered her life forever.

The last rays of sun were fading as Jean slowed the car, preparing for a left turn. Seeing nothing ahead, she crossed into the oncoming lane. Kathy thought she saw a blur on the horizon. "Watch out!" she cried, but her warning came too late.

Jean felt the impact smash through her body like a great sonic boom. It rattled her teeth as the oncoming car slammed into the passenger side of her car. The car spun around in a 360-degree arc, lurching to a stop. Jean struggled to regain her equilibrium. She could feel blood trickling down her forehead, and she felt as if the wind had been knocked out of her. But she was not alarmed until she suddenly realized that Kathy was no longer in the car with her.

Jean frantically scanned the shattered car. The entire right front section of the car had been smashed in. Blood and glass were splattered across the passenger seat. The door hung loosely on its hinges, a bent and twisted mouth, open, but telling nothing about the passenger it had just spit out.

Jean let out a low moan when she realized that Kathy had been thrown from the car.

"Are you okay?" someone asked. It was a male voice. A young man of about twenty was looking in at Jean as she struggled to open the car door.

"I'm... fine," she stammered. "My sister?"

"Yeah. I'm afraid she's hurt bad."

Jean's heart sank, yet instinctively a calming mechanism took over. *Mustn't panic,* she thought. *Got to stay calm. Help Kathy.*

"Call the police," she muttered. The young man, eager to do something, turned and ran down the street to call for help. How he and his friend had survived the crash unhurt was a mystery. Their car, about twenty feet down the road, had flipped over and the roof was crushed.

Slowly, with wooden steps, Jean made her way through broken glass and metal fragments to the other side of the car. There she found Kathy lying in the street, just off the edge of the sidewalk. Kathy's head lay in a puddle of blood. One leg was twisted and bent behind her. Her pants were ripped open at the knee, and she was bleeding there. She also had a dirty and jagged open wound on her right arm. Kathy was thrashing about, trying to sit up. She was moaning, a deep, low, animal-like sound, and then screaming, high-pitched and eerie.

Kathy's scream jarred Jean back to her senses. She ran over to her sister and took her by the shoulders, trying to hold her down. "Kathy, you're hurt. Please lie back down. We're sending for help."

Kathy spoke, but it was garbled, incomprehensible. *She's in shock,* thought Jean. *All this blood... Need a towel... In my car.* Jean cried out to the bystanders, "Someone get a towel, please, in my car. Did anyone call an ambulance?"

"They're on their way," someone said.

As Jean reached for the towel, Kathy let out another ear-piercing scream, then began to moan again.

"Kathy, please hang on," begged Jean as she began to wipe the blood from her sister's face. "The ambulance will be here soon; you'll be okay." But in her heart Jean was not so sure.

Kathy rolled her head. "Mnumm, nniumm... oowww..."

Jean reached under Kathy's head to still her. What she felt almost made her faint. Kathy's skull was not intact. There was a huge crack in the back of Kathy's head; part of her skull bone was broken off, exposing the delicate brain tissue.

"Oh, no. Please God, no," pleaded Jean. But it was too late, the damage had been done. *My sister is going to die,* thought Jean. *I know Kathy is going to die.*

With a roar of sirens, the ambulance finally arrived.

"It's okay miss. I'll take over now," a paramedic told Jean. Gently he released Jean's hands from Kathy's head and checked the damage to Kathy's skull. His eyes met Jean's for a moment, and Jean saw hopelessness written there. Reaching into his bag for a bandage, the paramedic wrapped it around Kathy's head. He put a collar around her neck to prevent any more movement. He checked Kathy's pupils for reaction to light. Shining a small flashlight into her eyes, he said that the right eye reacted sluggishly, suggesting an injury to the left side of the brain.

"What happened?" a man's voice demanded, breaking the silence. It was Bill. He had seen the ambulance as he left Phyl's Bar and had driven by. He knew that in a small town there was a chance he would know the victims of the accident. But he did not expect what he saw. "Kathy?" He could not believe his eyes. Here she was with her head bandaged and blood all around her, thrashing about, moaning, and screaming. "Kathy!" he yelled again. He wanted to go to her, but Jean held him back.

"Bill, there's nothing you can do right now. She won't recognize you; she's in shock. Let them get her to the hospital."

They watched as Kathy was moved onto a stretcher and loaded into the ambulance, her low moans giving way every few seconds to shrill screams. Bill would hear those screams in his dreams for a long time.

Jean touched Bill's shoulder. He looked so forlorn, so helpless.

"Bill, I'm going to ride in the ambulance with Kathy. Why don't you meet us at the hospital?"

"Of course," Bill muttered. Jean climbed in the back of the ambulance, and with its sirens wailing it sped away. Inside, Jean prayed, *God, please don't let my sister die.* But she wondered, *what will her life be like if she lives?*

While Kathy moaned, Jean shuddered and prayed.

15

Chapter 2

THE EMERGENCY ROOM

With sirens screeching and tires squealing, the ambulance roared up to the emergency entrance of the small hospital. The paramedics had called their dispatcher who relayed the message to the hospital–incoming trauma victim, head injury, emergency status of the highest priority.

The staff was waiting, As soon as the vehicle came to a stop, the rear doors were thrown open, and two men climbed aboard to transfer the gurney into the emergency room, where doctors and nurses scurried in all directions.

"Bring her over here," a doctor shouted. He was standing by a bed, next to a cart overflowing with emergency supplies–needles, medications, a heart monitor with defibrillator, oxygen, a respirator bag, and more.

Kathy was carefully transferred to the bed. A paramedic held her head steady at all times. Once Kathy was on the bed, a nurse began cutting her clothes off. Everything, blouse, bra, pants, was sheared and ripped apart to expose Kathy's body to their probing investigations.

"Right arm looks like it's broken," someone said. "Pretty dirty, too; may have to be debrided."

A nurse checked Kathy's vital signs,–heart rate, blood pressure, respiration. Her blood pressure was 94 over 60, which was good, considering the amount of blood she had lost. But her right pupil again responded sluggishly to light–left brain trauma.

"How's that knee look?" someone else asked.

"Knee's okay for now," came the reply. "May be a problem later, if she survives."

"Let's get this bandage off and take a look at the head injury," said the doctor in charge.

Slowly, carefully, a nurse began to unwrap Kathy's

bandaged head. As the last of the gauze came off, Kathy's fractured skull bones settled and spread open to expose the delicate pink tissue, peppered with dirt and gravel bits.

"Oh, God!" The nurse brought her hand to her mouth.

"Let's see," said the doctor, pushing her aside. "Hmmm. Doesn't look good at all. There's got to have been some damage here." He pointed to the region of Kathy's brain that was exposed and dirty. "It's starting to ooze, too. Let's get an x-ray, stat. And you might as well put the bandage back on," he said. "There's nothing we can do for her here. She'll have to be shipped out."

The paramedic stepped forward. "We can transfer her to the Toledo Trauma Center whenever you're ready, sir," he said.

"Good," answered the doctor "Just stand by. We'll get the x-ray and get her stabilized for the trip. In the meantime fill me in on what you have done so far."

The paramedic reported on the treatment given at the scene and during the ambulance ride. Meanwhile the doctor was cleaning the wounds on Kathy's arm and knee, removing as much dirt and grit as possible and putting fresh bandages on them. The nurses continued to check her vital signs, which remained stable. Kathy was still moaning, but she became conscious every now and then. Each time she did, she began to thrash about and had to be held down by the nurses.

"Ms. Hughes, Kathy, can you understand me?" A nurse looked into Kathy's eyes but they were vacant and wild.

"I don't think she's with it, doctor," she said.

"Not surprising," said the doctor. "Good. Here's x-ray. Move aside please. Let them in.

A large gray metal machine was being maneuvered into the emergency room. It admitted a shrill warning sound as it rolled forward. Guided from behind by a short, petite young woman, it loomed like a giant over Kathy's bed.

"Excuse me, please." The technician quickly went about her business, neither acknowledging nor ignoring the people gathered around. When she had placed the large rectangular metal plate containing the x-ray film under Kathy's head, the people moved away without having to be told.

The technician covered herself with a heavy leaded jacket to protect her from the x-rays. "Ready," she signaled and then pressed the button.

With the x-ray, the doctors could better evaluate Kathy's injury to determine its full extent and the measures needed to prevent further damage. For the time being, Kathy's biggest problem was that her damaged brain was starting to swell as indicated by the oozing of sticky fluid from the opening in her skull. If it swelled beyond the capacity of Kathy's skull, the pressures created could cause even further damage, not only in the injured area, but in other parts of her brain as well. Kathy's condition was critical.

The decision was obvious. The Port Clinton hospital clearly could not treat Kathy's injuries. In cases like this, the patient was given emergency care and stabilized, then taken either by ambulance or helicopter to a designated trauma center fifty miles away.

Kathy's vital signs continued to stabilize, and although the oozing persisted, she was not in immediate danger. The ambulance was ready.

"Let's get her back in there," said the doctor. "I'm calling the trauma center with a report. They'll be ready for you." He turned to one of the nurses. "You'll ride with them. Here's her chart and x-ray."

Once again Kathy was moved into the ambulance. It would be a fifty-minute ride to the trauma center.

Jean and Bill watched as Kathy's limp body was loaded into the ambulance. A nurse and a paramedic climbed in behind her. Jean moved toward the ambulance, but another paramedic stopped her.

"You may as well follow us in your friend's car," he said. "There's not much you can do in here."

Jean looked at Bill. He was pale and quiet. Kathy did not seem to need her now, but Bill did. "Okay" she said finally.

Bill was unusually subdued. He needed time to come to grips with what had happened.

"Like the man said, Jean," he started, licking his dry lips, "there's nothing we can do right now. She'll probably be in the ER at the center for a while before we can even see her. There's no need to rush down there."

He looked at Jean and then turned his eyes downward. "I don't know about you," he said. "But I could use a drink. What do you say we stop by Phyl's before we go to the trauma center?"

"Okay, Bill," said Jean quietly. "But you drive."

Doctor Brown had just made himself a sandwich of cold salami and cheese from the refrigerator in the doctor's lounge. He opened a can of juice and sat down with a sigh in front of the television. Then his beeper went off. "Dr. Brown to the ER, stat," it chirped.

"Never fails," he murmured as he grabbed a bite of sandwich and a gulp of juice on his way out. With his white coattails flying, he rushed into the hospital's trauma center.

"What have we got?" he asked the nurse at the desk.

"Head trauma coming in, sir. Bad one," she said. "I've got a call in to Dr. Andrews."

Dr. Brown was one of the ER physicians on call. It was his duty to be available all night long for emergencies, so he stayed in the hospital, sleeping and relaxing in the doctor's lounge when there was a lull in the activity. But in a busy trauma center, there was seldom time to relax. Car accidents, shootings, and other serious emergencies were routed here by police officers and paramedics on the scenes of the accidents. Also, the center was a regional referral center for patients from smaller hospitals, like the one Kathy had first been taken to. In addition to these more serious emergencies, the ER received "routine" emergencies, such as cuts, fractured limbs and croupy babies. On the average night, Dr. Brown saw fifty or more patients.

"Must be serious," said Dr. Brown, "if Andrews has been called in already."

Dr. Andrews was a neurosurgeon. Since most emergency cases did not require his specialized skills, he could spend his on-call hours away from the hospital, as long as he was within the beeper's range. However, in a case like Kathy's where a head injury with a skull fracture was involved, surgery was likely, and the doctor was called in. Everything needed to be ready so that no time would be lost.

Dr. Andrews arrived shortly before 10:30. "Tell surgery to prepare a room and stand by," he ordered, having already been briefed over the phone. "Do we have everything we need here?" He nodded towards the area that had been set up in preparation for Kathy's arrival.

"Yes sir," promised the nurse. She knew that Dr. Andrews was meticulously efficient. Any delays once the patient arrived that were due to poor preparation would not be tolerated. When the life of the patient depended on quick, efficient action, there was no room for errors caused by staff oversights.

"They're here," a nurse called out, and quickly Kathy was brought in, once again being transferred from the ambulance gurney to an ER bed.

Slightly more pale than before, Kathy was nonetheless alert this time, with her eyes open.

"Kathy, do you know where you are?" asked the nurse. Kathy responded with a moan and some gibberish.

"Communication impaired," said Dr. Andrews to the nurse taking notes.

"Blood pressure's down a little from the last reading," reported another nurse, taking new readings of Kathy's vital signs. All eyes were on Dr. Andrews as he began to carefully unwrap Kathy's bandages.

"Large laceration on the left temporoparietal region," he noted. "Depressed skull fracture; section of skull bone loose and free floating. Wound oozing profusely. Bits of white, brain-like material outside of skull area." He looked up. "How's her pupil reaction?"

"Pupils round and equal, reacting to light," said Dr. Brown, who was examining Kathy's other injuries. "She seems able to move all extremities, but the left side is better than the right. There is no obvious paralysis of the face, arms, or legs at this time."

"Good," said Dr. Andrews, having seen all he needed. "Let's get this woman to surgery. Is the family around?"

"They were following us, sir." said a paramedic.

A nurse went to the reception area and returned a few moments later.

"They've just arrived," she said.

"Give them the consent papers, and then let's move," he ordered. "I'll speak to the family, and then I'll be in the scrub room when you're ready."

ℰ--------------------℃ℛ

Jean pushed her bangs out of her eyes for the fourth time in five minutes and patted her foot anxiously.

"Do we have to answer these questions *now*, nurse?" she asked.

"Yes, I'm afraid so," came the antiseptic reply.

Good grief, thought Jean. *Here I am, wondering if my sister is going to live or not, and they are asking about insurance. Who cares about insurance at a time like this? And what's taking that doctor so long, anyway?*

"Just give me your insurance card, Jean," Bill said. "I'll finish up. Why don't you sit down for a while?"

"I can't," said Jean. But she fished the card out of her purse, handed it to Bill, and turned away. *Well, God,* she thought, *if you were ever going to do me a favor—now's the time.*

21

"Ms. Hughes?" Jean turned around to see a man approaching her, wearing a white hospital jacket over street clothes.

"Hi," he said, extending his arm. "I'm Dr. Andrews. I've just seen your sister. She's in stable condition right now, but she has a big problem, as you know. Her head injury appears to have caused damage to some brain tissue. How much I won't know until I can take a closer look. That means surgery, of course. She's got to have that wound cleaned out, and we'll have to repair some of the lining that covers her brain. There's also a piece of skull bone that is completely broken off–it will have to be removed. I'm afraid that she's had one heck of a bump on the head."

Jean looked down at the floor. "What are her chances?" she asked.

"Oh, I *think* she'll come through it okay, but... well... there might be some loss of brain function."

Jean's head jerked up. "What kind of loss? How much?"

"I'm sorry Ms. Hughes, I can't answer that with any certainty. All I can tell you is that at present we find some loss of motor control of the right leg and arm, although she is moving these extremities. I am hopeful that after surgery she will retain at least as much function in these parts as she has now. But neurologically–as far as her brain function is concerned–it's hard to say. When you're dealing with someone's brain you never know for sure what to expect. There is evidence of trauma to the brain itself, but at present it appears to be localized in the lower left quadrant. This would indicate to me that we can expect some loss of speech and language facility, since this is the area of the brain from which those functions originate."

"You're saying she could have some trouble talking..., like.., like with that... babbling she's been doing?" Jean stammered.

"Yes, *exactly*," said the doctor. "And many patients also have difficulty with comprehension as well. But that's a

22

bridge to be crossed later. I just wanted to forewarn you that it will likely be a difficult recovery. By the way, have her parents been notified?"

"No, I wanted to wait," started Jean, *"to see..."* Jean's voice trailed off as she thought to herself, *I haven't had the courage to tell them.*

"Why don't you call right now? There's a phone over on that wall." Dr. Andrews pointed to the wall opposite them.

"Okay," said Jean, "but would you stay here a moment? My dad might want to talk to you. He's a doctor himself. He'll want to know the details."

"Sure," said Dr. Andrews gently as he turned aside and motioned for a nurse to come over to him. "Bring me the chart on Kathy Hughes."

℘--------------------☙

Jean's father sounded sleepy as he answered the phone. It was after midnight in St. Louis.

"Dad ..." Jean's voice was a hoarse whisper. "Dad, there's been an accident. I'm okay, but it's Kathy." Jean's throat tightened as she fought back the flood of tears that she knew, once started, would not easily stop. Biting her lip, she turned to Dr. Andrews and silently handed him the phone.

"Dr. Hughes, this is Dr. Andrews."

Jean caught bits and pieces of the conversation–" ... left parietal skull fracture... contusion... jagged bone and dirt...laceration... left temporoparietal region... surgery... nothing you can do."–, but her brain was pounding with a trauma of its own, the trauma of acknowledging that her sister would never be the same again. The Kathy she knew–the spunky childhood pal, the fun-loving, free spirited individualist–was gone, perhaps forever.

But if Kathy wasn't Kathy anymore, who *or what* would she become? Jean shuddered as she recalled the accident scene with vivid horror and Kathy in a pool of blood, her head open, brain exposed, moaning that low, animal moan.

"Ms. Hughes..." The doctor's voice brought Jean back to the lobby. "I'm going to scrub for surgery now; I'll be out to talk to you as soon as we are done. I told your father there was no need for him to come tonight. There's nothing he can do here. We'll call him in the morning. I need you to sign these papers–consent for surgery."

Jean took the clipboard the doctor handed her and signed the papers without reading them.

"Try to get some rest," the doctor said as he left her.

Sure, rest, thought Jean as she watched the white–coated figure walk briskly down the hail and disappear, *I don't know that I'll ever rest again.*

She placed the palms of her hands over her throbbing temples. She began to think back to her childhood. *All those years in Catholic school, reciting verses and saying prayers,* she thought. *I've prayed to God all of my life, but it was just rote memorization much of the time. Now that I really need to communicate with God, I hope he's listening. Dear God,* she started. As the minutes ticked by, Jean prayed in earnest, asking for a miracle.

Chapter 3

COMING TO REALITY

The nurse wiped away the beads of sweat that were forming on Dr. Andrews' brow as he concentrated on his intricate work. He had been at it for five hours. It would probably take five more. *God, what a mess,* he thought to himself. *I've never seen anything like it outside of a war zone.* Bit by bit he removed the smashed bone, dirt, and gravel from Kathy's brain, delicately, carefully trying to disturb as little of the vulnerable pink brain tissue as possible. Still, he knew some tissue would be lost.

Kathy's vital signs were being carefully monitored during the long operation. Whenever her pulse or blood pressure started to drop, the anesthesiologist carefully readjusted the mixture of oxygen, nitrogen, and the gases being used to keep Kathy unconscious. She was far removed from the operating room and the drama surrounding her.

Kathy slowly rose to a state of awareness. She felt disoriented at first, but then began to focus. She looked around her. There was a blinding sunshine infused in every inch of space as far as she could see. She suddenly became aware of voices. There were people, people everywhere talking, laughing, joyous, but she could not quite make out the voices. There was something strange about them. They were *floating.* Kathy tried hard to concentrate, but she could not. The hazy, translucent figures continued to visit with one another, oblivious to Kathy's presence.

Where am I? She wondered, awestruck. *Did I die? Is this heaven?* She became aware for the first time of the peacefulness of the place. *If this is heaven,* she thought, *I*

25

love it. It's so serene, so calm. I feel at peace, and it's wonderful. It's bliss. Kathy sighed and basked in the serene atmosphere, for how long she did not know–maybe a few minutes, perhaps a few days. Time had no meaning.

She looked into the faces of the people around her, yet she saw no one she knew. No one spoke to her. *Are they angels, perhaps saints?* She wondered. *If this is heaven, I'd like to see more of it.* But another thought intruded.

Yes, it is wonderful here, but earth is good too. I love my friends, my family. I love Bill. Suddenly Kathy felt torn. She knew that if she stayed much longer, she would not be able to go back. But did she want to go back, and could she give up this feeling of total bliss?

Without seeing him, Kathy became aware that a supreme being, God, was with her. She felt him reach out to her to comfort and guide her in this decision.

I don't know what to do, Kathy told him, *I can't decide. I love the earth and I love it here. Please, you decide for me.*

She heard no voice but a resounding message was instantly communicated to her.

Kathy, go back. I'm not finished with you yet.

Amidst the glare of fluorescent lights, Kathy awoke in her hospital bed, having returned once again to the world of the living.

Chapter 4

SHATTERED DREAMS

Kathy blinked and tried to turn away from the glare of the lights. She was still feeling peaceful, contented, and serene. She wanted to hold on to that feeling, but the sound of a familiar voice distracted her.

"Kathy." She heard her name called again. "Kathy, it's Mom. I'm here. Kathy, you've been in an accident."

Kathy's mind snapped to attention. *Mom? What is my mother doing here all the way from St. Louis? And what is it that she was saying—an accident?*

"You're going to be okay," her mother was continuing. "But it's going to take some time."

Time? Time for what? Kathy wondered. *Where am I?* She tried to sit up, but she barely got her head off the pillow. She was so tired. She just wanted to drift off, to sleep, or maybe to find that beautiful, peaceful place again.

But she could not. There was something wrong. If she could just think—something to do with her mother. Her mother? Kathy's mind would not stay put. It seemed to be drifting in and out. If only she could focus, concentrate.

Mom? Kathy tried to speak her mother's name but she could not make a sound. There was something in her throat, blocking her vocal cords, choking her. She gagged and tried again, struggling against the tube.

Kathy's mother lifted her. Kathy saw the pained look on her face, and the way she was gritting her teeth, trying not to show it.

What's wrong Mom? Kathy's mind cried out, but no words came. She was helpless. *What is this thing? Why can't I talk?* Kathy wondered. *A little while ago everything was so peaceful, so calm and serene. Now everything is all mixed up, and I don't understand what's going on.*

"Kathy," her mother said, trying to answer the questions in her daughter's eyes. "Kathy, you're in the hospital. You and Jean were in an accident–a car wreck. Jean's okay, but... but you were hurt. You need to take it easy and rest. Then everything will be okay."

A hospital? Kathy's mind revolted at the thought. *No! Hospitals are for sick people,* she thought. *I'm not sick. I've got to get out of here. I want to go home. I want to see Bill. Bill! Where's Bill?* Kathy struggled to free herself of the gigantic weight that seemed to be holding her down, pinning her to the bed. Tears formed in her eyes as she realized it was useless. *I'm not going to stand for this,* she thought. *I'll get out. I'll show them. Soon...very soon.* But gradually the frustration and confusion faded away, and she drifted into a dreamless sleep.

Virginia Hughes watched her daughter fall back into a semiconscious state. *It's just as well,* she thought, as she brushed away the tears from her eyes. She had hardly recognized her daughter when she entered the ICU earlier that day. In fact, she had walked right by her room. She was braced for a shock, having been warned by Dr. Andrews that Kathy's face would be swollen and her head wrapped from the surgery. But when the nurse took her arm and directed her to Kathy's bed, she almost fainted. This person with the terrible black and blue marks, the horribly swollen face, *that* was her daughter? She watched the girl struggle helplessly against the breathing tube that seemed to be choking her. It extended from her mouth, where it was connected to the oxygen equipment, all the way down her throat and into her lungs. There were needles taped to her arms, connecting her to the I.V. bottles that hung in rows above her bed, some of them piggy-backed one on top of the other. A giant turban of bandages covered her entire head. It was hard to believe *this* was Kathy.

Virginia Hughes had been through many accidents with her twelve kids. The inevitable cuts, scrapes, and broken bones seemed to be a part of growing up. But they had been lucky–until now. Being a doctor's wife, she had always been aware of tragedies that could happen, but somehow her family had been spared any major traumas–until now.

And why Kathy–Kathy, of all of them, of anyone? Kathy was so in love with freedom, with independence. Why did God choose to restrict Kathy so severely? The doctor told Virginia the prognosis. There were no promises, only questions.

You've always been a fighter, Kathy, she thought. *Well, now you're in for the fight of your life.*

She slumped down into the chair next to her daughter's bed. The enormity of the situation overwhelmed her, and she dropped her head into her hands and cried for her daughter, for herself, for her family. She knew they would all suffer for a long time to come.

"Mom?" A hand was on Virginia's shoulder, and she looked up, wiping away her tears. It was Beth, one of her younger daughters. Beth had always been close to Kathy.

"I came as soon as I heard," Beth said. She had made the trip from St. Louis to be with her sister, fearing what she might find, but compelled to be there. Mother and daughter embraced, their bonds of love increased by their common concern.

"How is she?" Beth asked. "Has she woken up yet?"

"Only for moments at a time," replied her mother. "When she does, she struggles and gags. It's so sad." Kathy's mother looked away and Beth touched her shoulder once again.

"At least she's alive. We can be thankful for that. Kathy's a fighter. She'll come back."

Tense hours passed as other members of Kathy's family gathered by her side. Kathy, oblivious to their concern and worry, was blissfully drifting in a world of her own.

Two days passed before Kathy regained consciousness.

As she opened her eyes, she saw her mother and immediately started to cry. She knows, thought Virginia. She knows, and now the real pain begins. Finally freed of the restrictive breathing tube, Kathy was anxious to communicate, to find out exactly what had happened to her.

"Blizerumph?" Kathy said, but her mother did not respond. "Blizerumph?" she tried again. Why wouldn't her mother answer?

"Kathy, don't try to talk," her mother finally said. "Just rest. Your speech will get better soon. Then we can talk."

There's nothing wrong with my speech, thought Kathy, beginning to get irritated. *And I want to talk now! I want some answers. Don't tune me out! Damnit, look at me!* Kathy spewed out a string of four letter words.

"Kathy!" Her mother was shocked. "That's not like you."

She looks surprised, thought Kathy. *Got your attention, didn't I?*

"It's okay, Mrs. Hughes." A nurse had entered the room. "This happens quite often," she explained. "When the speech centers of the brain are damaged and the patient can't communicate, the frustration often triggers other centers of the brain. Cursing is not an everyday form of communication for most of us, so perhaps the memory of these words is stored elsewhere, in a part of her brain that was not damaged. It's amazing what patients will drag up. If they can't communicate in normal language, they will speak to us in whatever way they can."

So it was to be. It became evident that Kathy could use little or no normal language. But she could sing. She sang songs she had learned in grade school. She recited nursery rhymes and a few bits of old sayings. "Okay, dokey, Smokey" seemed to be her favorite. And she cursed-and cursed.

During the next forty-eight hours Kathy tried several times to communicate, but her words were gibberish, incomprehensible. After a while she seemed to give up trying to make herself understood. She withdrew into her own, inner world and often had a glazed look in her eyes when others spoke to her. She seldom responded to family members other than her mother. But she did respond to Bill. He had remained close by, and whenever he was allowed into ICU to visit, he tried to get Kathy to respond to his voice. The nurses had told both him and the family that Kathy would require almost constant stimulation if she was to regain her faculties. And Kathy reacted most to Bill's voice.

℘--------------------Cℜ

It was quiet in ICU when Virginia was aroused out of a nap by the beeping of an approaching x-ray machine.

"For Kathy?" she asked as the young technician stopped in her vicinity.

"Yes, ma'am," replied the girl. "I'll need to get a little closer."

"Oh, of course." Kathy's mother moved her chair away from the bed and took a seat across from where the girl was working. She watched as the technician turned dials and adjusted the large arm of the machine, positioning it over Kathy's prone body. When she had the machine correctly adjusted, the technician called a nurse over to help her lift Kathy onto the metal plate containing the x-ray film. Kathy was asleep and only murmured a small protest as the two grabbed her under the armpits and hoisted her up and onto the plate.

"Okay, that's it," said the technician. Then she remembered something. "Almost forgot," she added as she went to her machine and returned with a leaded coverlet, which she then placed over Kathy's stomach area.

"What's that for?" asked Kathy's mom.

"Oh, it's just protection for the baby from the x-rays when we take the picture," explained the girl.

"Baby!? What baby?" demanded Kathy's mother,

31

suddenly on her feet. "What on earth are you talking about?"

"Oh, I'm sorry," said the girl sheepishly. "I thought you knew." She looked at the nurse, who was giving her an acid glare. "I'm sorry," she repeated.

"Mrs. Hughes..." the nurse started.

"Oh, no, this can't be true," cried Virginia. "Not a *baby* on top of it all! My God, why didn't anyone tell me? Why am I the last to *know?*"

For a few moments there was silence. Then Virginia Hughes' anguished sobs broke the spell. She retreated to the far corner of the room, where she sank into a chair, crying openly–a defeated, hopeless sound.

છૅ---------------------ૡ

Bill tiptoed quietly into the room. He had been warned by the nurse that the secret was out. He knew he had some explaining to do, and he was aware that even with his easy charm, he would not be able to talk his way out of this one.

"Hello, Bill. I've been waiting for you."

He tensed at the sound of Virginia's voice, which seemed to be made of ice.

"Bill, when did this happen? Why didn't you tell me?" she asked.

"I'm really sorry, Mrs. Hughes," Bill said, looking down at the floor "We were going to tell you, soon, but... well... you know, there were things we wanted to discuss first. And then the accident happened. After that, there never seemed to be a good time to bring it up."

"Who else knew?"

"Only Jean," said Bill. "And then I told the nurses, at the hospital, in the emergency room. I thought they should know."

"Of course," said Kathy's mother, saddened that it had not occurred to him in all this time that perhaps she should know also. Virginia sighed. *Even in the best circumstances, this would be a problem. But now... Oh well,* she thought.

What's done is done. The baby's a reality, so there's nothing to do but hope for the best. Now I have two lives to pray for, she thought.

She looked at Bill. He looked like a sixth-grader who had been called in to the principal's office.

"Oh, Bill," she said, holding out her arms. "It's okay. We're a family now. We're in this together."

Bill gratefully accepted the hug.

Chapter 5

THE STRUGGLE TO RECOVER BEGINS

Before long Kathy was waking up at regular intervals. It had been five days since her surgery, and she had accepted the fact that she was in the hospital. She was beginning to recognize her family members, even though at times her mind seemed to shut down, and she became lost or confused in her thinking. Generally, if something was interesting, she would try to pay attention, at least for a short time. Otherwise, her mind took her off on pleasant but disorienting "sentimental journeys." Past and present sometimes blended. Time had no meaning in Kathy's private world.

But as her awareness increased, Kathy's anger and frustration was also growing. Irritation finally gave way to frenzied agitation when time after time Kathy tried in vain to make herself understood. What really frustrated her was when she asked a simple, straight-forward question and people looked at her as if she had spoken Greek. Were they just not listening or *what?* And when they asked *her* a question, her answers never seemed to satisfy them. They always wanted something different, something more. It got so confusing and so tiring. Kathy could never remember being more tired in her life.

Kathy's major frustration was in not being able to express the turbulent feelings she was experiencing. Her many visitors seemed to exist in a reality that was slightly removed from hers. They could not easily enter her world, and it seemed she could not enter theirs–except for Bill. Kathy could recognize the sound of Bill's voice, and she knew his special touch. She would have preferred that everybody else just leave her alone. He was the only visitor she wanted to see. It was Bill she longed for, Bill who filled her waking thoughts and her dreams.

℘--------------------℘

It was hot in the bar. Kathy looked over at her sister Jean. "Want another drink, or should we go back to the cottage?" she asked.

"We've only got ten more days of vacation left here in Catawba," said Jean. "I want to make the most of them. Let's stay awhile longer."

"Whatever you say, Jean."

Kathy had felt like socializing when they first entered the bar an hour ago and her eyes once again scanned the tiny tavern for signs of summer friends, regulars like herself who came here year after year to vacation on Lake Erie's beautiful Catawba Island. But tonight the usually friendly bar seemed distant, lonely. It was half empty, and the people there were strangers to Kathy and Jean.

Just then the door opened, and Kathy's heart skipped a beat. She took a long look at the handsome stranger who had just entered. His manner was arresting. His eyes were compelling. He seemed rugged, yet charismatic as he nodded an acknowledgement to Kathy's stare and then casually slipped onto a barstool.

Kathy was in a panic. This was *he*, the man of her dreams. She felt it instantly. She knew it instinctively. *This is too much,* she thought. *I've got to calm down and get hold of my emotions. He's just a stranger. I don't know anything about him. But my instincts are never wrong. I know this man is going to become a part of my life. Am I ready for this?*

"Excuse me, Jean. I have to go to the bathroom." Shaking inside, Kathy made her way past the bar. She dared not look in the direction of the stranger. Inside the restroom her head argued with her heart. *Let it go,* she thought. *You've only got ten more days till summer vacation is over. Why start something up now?* Yet she could not ignore the intense attraction. Torn, she finally resorted to her favorite decision making tactic. *I'll let it go, do nothing, and whatever is meant to happen will happen,* she thought.

Satisfied with this logic, Kathy left the restroom. She almost gasped aloud as she looked over and saw Jean at the bar, talking to the handsome stranger. *There's no turning back now,* she thought, as on rubbery legs she walked headlong into her fate.

"Kathy, this is Bill. Bill, my sister, Kathy."

The rest was a whirlwind of emotion, a kaleidoscope of images. They talked for two hours at the bar. Kathy hardly noticed that Jean was still there, waiting patiently for her. When they finally stood up to leave, Kathy had impulsively invited Bill to join them for a picnic at the family cottage the following day.

"Kathy, are you sure you know what you're doing?" Jean asked, giving her sister a quizzical look. "I've never been more sure of anything in my life," said Kathy.

∞--------------------∞

The whole family was there for the picnic. Bill appeared to be somewhat overwhelmed by the sheer number of Kathy's brothers and sisters, not to mention the nieces and nephews.

"When you say a family picnic, you really mean *family,* don't you?" he kidded her, trying to hide a slight tension in his voice.

"Does it bother you? We can leave, you know," Kathy said. She had forgotten about the unsettling effect that her large family sometimes had on people.

"Oh, no, I didn't mean that," Bill assured her. "I'll get used to it. It's just that I'm not normally what you'd call a real sociable person. I guess I don't like small talk."

"No problem," said Kathy. "I don't like small talk either. Let's swim!" She grabbed his arm and pulled him toward the beach.

Laughing, Bill followed Kathy down to the shore where white foamy bubbles rolled and tumbled atop gently breaking waves. As soon as their feet touched the water, Bill spun around and grabbed Kathy, lifting her into the air.

"Oh, no you don't," she cried, trying to wiggle out of his arms. But before she could free herself, Bill went out into the waves, and, throwing himself into an on-coming breaker, drenched them both.

"I'll get you for that! Kathy squealed as she pushed back her wet hair. "Come here." She tried to pull Bill down into the water, but he was too strong. Instead he pulled her toward him and took Kathy's face in both his hands.

"Face it, you're no match for me," he said quietly. As he covered her mouth with a kiss, Kathy knew he was right. She was in his control.

That evening they built a bonfire on the beach. Kathy snuggled into the crook of Bill's arm and was more content than she could ever remember. Right here and now she had it all. What more could there be?

They talked long into the night. Gradually the family members had said good night and drifted off to bed. The fire had burned down to a few red, glowing embers. Kathy had wrapped a blanket around herself and Bill. They huddled close for warmth, enjoying the touch of each other's bodies.

Going back through her childhood memories, Kathy told Bill things she had never told anyone else. He had that effect on her. He drew her out, made her want to bare her soul, but only to him. His eyes were mesmerizing, hypnotizing. As he gazed into her face, she could feel him searching out her secret places. But she didn't care. She was falling in love, head over heels, as she never had before.

"Well, what about you?" Kathy finally asked. "Now that you know everything about me, it's your turn," she challenged.

"I guess I'm a bit of a loner, too," he said. "We have a lot in common. We're both party people. We like to have a good time. But we're kind of private about our personal lives. We don't often share that side of ourselves."

"Except with someone special," Kathy whispered.

"Yes, except with someone special," he answered as he took her into his arms, putting an end to her questions with his kiss.

The ten days flew by. Kathy hardly noticed one day fading into the next. She was walking on air, completely consumed by thoughts of Bill. They spent most of their time together, and Kathy was content to let herself pretend it would never end.

But the vacation did end. The family packed up and closed the cottage.

"I'm staying here," Kathy announced. "I'm not going back to St. Louis with you. I'm going to stay and work in Port Clinton for a while."

"Well, Kathy," her father said, "I guess that's up to you." He threw a concerned look in Bill's direction, but Bill did not speak.

"Yes it is up to me," Kathy said. "I'm finished with school. I can look for a job in social work here, and in the meantime, I have a bartending job lined up."

"Well, it sounds like you've given it some thought," Kathy's mother said.

"Yes, I have," said Kathy. "I know what I'm doing."

Three months later, Kathy was in a quandary. She had been offered a good job in social work with the Aid for Dependent Children program in Sandusky, Ohio. It was not that far away, but if she accepted the job, she would not be able to see Bill as often as she did now. She wanted to see more, not less of him. Still, it was a good opportunity for starting her career in the field for which she had trained. She thought she probably should take it.

Bill was not as upset as Kathy thought he might be.

"It's okay, honey," he assured her. "We'll see each

other lots. Don't worry. I won't let a little driving get between me and my special girl."

"Special girl?" Kathy thought about those words. Did he mean special as in "one and only" or special among the girls he was seeing? She wondered if Bill had been with other girls since she moved to Port Clinton. Perhaps she had been too hasty in her decision to move here. But whenever she broached the subject with him, Bill hedged.

"You know no on else means anything to me," he told her. "You're the one I really care about."

But somehow, Kathy did not feel that Bill was committed to their relationship. *Okay,* she thought, *I understand. Maybe we both need some space—a little distance between us might be a good thing. Bill can decide once and for all what he really wants from this relationship.*

Kathy moved to Sandusky and threw herself into her new job, concentrating on establishing her career. As she had feared, Bill became more distant over time. He was pulling away from her.

Three years went by. Kathy became a competent and confident social worker. She kept in close contact with her family, writing and calling often. One letter from a sister told Kathy of a great job opening in St. Louis, at St. John's Hospital, and suggested that Kathy move back home near her family. They all missed her.

It was a great opportunity, and Kathy knew it was the right move to make. As a social worker in the orthopedic and rehabilitation department of the hospital, she would work directly with patients who had suffered severe trauma, helping them to put their lives back together. Kathy took the job. Little did she know that a mere two years later, she herself would become one of these patients.

Kathy enjoyed her new job. She had a genuine concern for others, and she cared deeply for her patients. Their misfortunes saddened her, but this made her try all the harder to find a way to be of service to them. She gave them moral as well as professional support, easing their reentry into the mainstream of life.

Then came the phone call. Bill had been thinking about her. Was she coming to Catawba this summer? Kathy hesitated. It had been a long time. Would the energy still be there? Should she rekindle the fire? Then the memory of Bill's smile captured Kathy's adventurous spirit. Yes, she would be there.

Kathy went back to Catawba and spent a breathtaking week being swept off her feet once again by Bill's charms. He seemed to have grown even more handsome since she had last seen him. He seemed to have settled down, too. He was seriously working at starting his own construction business. *Maybe things will turn out differently this time,* Kathy thought.

Bill did appear to be more committed to her. He talked of his future and hinted that he wanted Kathy to be a part of it. When the vacation ended, and it was time for Kathy to leave again, Bill made her promise to return again soon for a weekend visit.

Within a few weeks they were traveling the five hundred miles back and forth between St, Louis and Port Clinton every weekend, taking turns. This long distance affair continued for six months, this time growing stronger with each reunion. Bill told Kathy he wanted her to be near again. He wanted to be able to see her more often and more easily. He told her he was serious about their relationship.

Once again, Kathy followed her heart. She gave her notice at the hospital in St. Louis. She returned to Port Clinton, determined to make it work this time. Bill would commit to her without reservation. She knew it. It might take time, but she could wait. She had plenty of time. Content with the direction their relationship was going, Kathy thought that all her dreams would come true.

As she lay in the hospital bed, Kathy's mind seemed to prefer these happy memories to reality. She vacillated between never wanting to leave these blissful memories and the desire to reach out to the real Bill, the Bill she somehow sensed was at her side, coaxing her, pleading with her to try to listen and understand. For Bill, she would try. For Bill she would make sense of this mishmash of reality and fantasy and regain her mastery of her world, *their* world.

Kathy moaned, a deep low protest to the pain that was intruding into her peaceful memories. "Ohhh." *Something hurting me... such pain... my stomach... cramps...* Kathy tried to turn over on her stomach to get some relief, but her arms were pinned down, tied to the side rails of her hospital bed. *Damn!* The frustration only increased her pain. Angrily she tried to release herself from the bondage of the arm restraints.

"Kathy, what's wrong?" her mother asked, concerned about her daughter's sudden thrashing. Kathy had been quiet the past two days, sleeping most of the time, but today she seemed restless, almost as though she was in pain.

Kathy moaned again, louder. *She is in pain,* thought her mother, *I wonder what could be hurting her?* She pulled the string that was attached to the nurses' call button.

"Someone please come in right away," she begged when they answered. "Something's wrong with Kathy."

Two nurses rushed in, stethoscopes in their hands, one immediately reaching for the blood pressure cuff, the other bending over Kathy to listen to her heartbeat.

"What seems to be the problem?" one nurse asked.

"I don't know," said Virginia. "She started thrashing around and moaning just a few moments ago, like she's in pain or something."

"Well, we'll check her. Why don't you wait outside?"

"No!" cried Virginia. "I want to be here."

"Okay, I understand," the nurse relented. "But please wait over there." She pointed to a chair by the window.

"Of course," said Virginia lamely, feeling brushed aside once again.

The nurse began checking Kathy's body for signs of a problem. Since brain injury typically causes no pain (brain tissue has no nerve endings), they were surprised at Kathy's discomfort. Eight days after surgery it was even more unusual.

Then they pulled back the sheet and saw it. A small stream of dark red blood was oozing out between Kathy's legs, making a bright stain on the sheets.

"Oh, my God," said one nurse. "In all the trauma, I forgot–the baby!"

"The baby? Oh, no!" cried Virginia.

"Mrs. Hughes, I'm sorry. But we have to act fast here. Please wait outside. We'll do whatever we can to save Kathy's baby." She had pushed the call button and now she turned her gaze away from Virginia's anguished face to bark out orders to the nurse at the desk.

"Call Dr. Andrews, stat, and Dr. Gentry. And then call O.B. and tell them to prepare a delivery room. I think Kathy Hughes is aborting!"

Kathy, looking pale and white, was being wheeled down the hall toward the delivery room. Bill managed to rush up to her side and race along beside her for a few steps. They stopped for a moment at the delivery room door.

"Kathy," Bill pleaded. "Kathy, listen to me. There will be other babies. Just get well. Please, just get well." Somewhere deep inside, Kathy rallied at the sound of Bill's voice.

Just get better... Bill says other babies. Just get better. Okay, Bill, for you I will get better. I must... for Bill.

Then she was gone, disappearing behind the swinging doors. But those words–Bills' words–would stay with Kathy forever.

Chapter 6

FULL REALIZATION COMES

The night nurse had just left Kathy's room, having finished her four A.M. rounds. Kathy was resting quietly, listening to the sounds of the busy intensive care ward. She heard the rhythmic "bleep, bleep" of the heart monitors, the hypnotic whoosh of a respirator. Kathy had awakened quite alert, the fog that normally clouded her thoughts having lifted for a while.

She moved slightly and felt the tug of her arm restraints. *Hey, I'm stuck here,* she thought. *Help! Somebody help me!* Kathy called out, but her words were gibberish, and no one answered her plea. Angry and frustrated, Kathy wiggled and twisted her arm inside the wrist restraint. Feeling it loosen slightly, she began to wiggle in earnest. She worked the thick cloth wrapping, pushing, pulling, tugging, twisting. Inch by inch she worked the restraint higher up on her arm. Finally, she felt her hand and wrist move freely. Kathy rotated her hand, easing the tension in the muscles. It felt great. But she was still stuck. Even though she had more mobility with the wrist restraint pushed up onto her forearm, she still could not lift her hand more than a few inches off the bed.

Patting the bed, Kathy's hand found the strips of bandaging that were connected to her wrist restraints. She followed the path with her hand until she felt the knots where they were attached to the bedsprings. Now, thought Kathy, as she began to work on the knots, *I'm going to get out of here... hospital's for sick people... not for me... got to get home... go back to work... see Bill.*

With single-minded determination, Kathy put all her strength into the effort. Pinching the knots with her fingernails, digging in, tugging, picking at the knots.

43

Minutes passed, a half-hour. Kathy continued to work, oblivious to the amount of time or energy she was using. Her mind was focused on a single goal–escape.

Finally the first knot gave way. *Got it!* thought Kathy. *Just a little more now.* The second knot was looser. Kathy untied it in only a few minutes. *Now I'm getting out of here,* thought Kathy. *I'm going home.*

One hand free, Kathy quickly used it to untie the other. She rested a moment, breathing a sigh of relief. It felt so good to move her arms about–up, down, across her chest. And to be able to turn over when *she* wanted to, not when somebody finally remembered to do it for her.

Turning onto her side, Kathy prepared to make her exit. *I'm getting out.* She swung one leg over the side of the bed, feeling its weight pull her closer to the edge. Taking a deep breath, Kathy swung the other leg over and, using one hand, pulled herself up and off the bed.

For a moment she just stood there. Getting her balance was not easy after lying flat in bed for more than a week. Tentatively, carefully, Kathy took a first wobbly step, leaning onto the side of the bed for support. She felt something tugging at her arm inside her elbow. It was her I.V., taped to her arm.

Don't need that anymore, she thought. *Going home.* She picked at the edges of the tape that held the I.V. needle in place. She loosened it enough to get her fingers under it. In one big jerk, Kathy ripped the I.V. out of her arm, throwing the needle and tubing across the bed.

Blood trickled out from the vein, dripping down onto the floor, but she did not care. Shaking now, she put one foot in front of the other and moved away from the bed. Suddenly free of support, Kathy felt heavy, awkward. She hesitated, tottered, looked down at the blood on her gown, and fell into a crumpled heap onto the floor.

"Kathy!" A nurse came running into her room, quickly followed by two more. "Kathy, where on earth do you think you're going?" the nurse yelled. "You can't get out of bed.

You're sick. Look at you! You're bleeding all over." Kathy understood little of what the nurse was saying. The words were coming too fast. But the word "blood" did register. Kathy knew blood. It was red and sticky and it came when you got hurt. Kathy saw the red blood on the floor, on the bed, on her gown. She started to cry. This meant she was not going home.

"It's okay, Kathy," a nurse said soothingly. "We'll take care of it. You just get back into bed like a good girl. We'll clean you up and fix your I.V. Then we'll give you fresh sheets. Here, just lie back down and relax now. You're okay."

The nurses moved quickly and efficiently, tidying up the room and cleaning the quickly drying blood off Kathy.

"We're going to have to tie your arms again, Kathy," a nurse said. "We can't have you hurting yourself again." She gave Kathy a look that was both sympathetic and stern at the same time.

"Keep an eye on her," she muttered as she passed by a coworker on her way out.

Defeated, Kathy spent the rest of the day vacillating between depression and angry determination. The episode only served to demonstrate just how helpless she was. Kathy could not understand why the nurse kept insisting she was sick. Kathy knew that any day now the fog that had settled in over her brain would lift permanently, and she would regain her speech. And the trouble she sometimes had understanding people would pass, too. It was only temporary. Then she would get back to work. Why, they must be swamped at work after taking over her caseload. Kathy sighed. So much to do. But she supposed it would have to wait, at least until she got her strength back. In the meantime she would not give up. *They may be able to slow me down,* she thought, *but nobody can stop Kathy Hughes when she sets her mind on something.*

For several days Kathy did just what she was told, waiting for her chance. "Eat, eat," they were always telling her, but she had not felt like eating. She had lost thirty pounds, and was glad to do it. She had always had to watch her weight, and she had weighed 135 lbs. just before the accident, more than she had ever weighed before. *Why eat when I'm not hungry?* She had thought.

But her weakness during her brief walk had shocked her. *I wouldn't have fallen if I had been stronger,* she thought. So Kathy ate. She ate when she was not hungry. She ate when she did not like the food. She ate to get stronger, to be in control of her body again.

"You're eating so well now, Kathy," the doctor said one day (as if eating was a big accomplishment). "So well, in fact," he said, "that we can take the I.V. out of your arm." She did not need supplemental intravenous feedings any longer. "But, I'm afraid we'll have to keep the restraints on a little longer," he said, 'just in case you forget where you are again and try to get out of bed. We can't have that happening, now can we?" He smiled that hospital smile that was supposed to communicate, "We're just doing this for your own good." Kathy did not respond.

Her mind was more alert each day. Even though her communication with others was almost nil, Kathy maintained a steady stream of conversation in her own head. Mostly she thought of Bill–and of going home, home to her cottage on the lake, where she could come and go as she pleased.

Kathy began to plan another escape. She forced herself to become oriented to time and place once again. Up to this point, Kathy had been drifting in an eternal now, where fantasy and reality converged and time was neither meaningful nor necessary. But Kathy realized that the people around her were relating to time schedules. They often asked her if she knew what day it was, or whether it was day or night. Kathy was vaguely aware that these subtleties of time and place existed and that they had been important to her too–once. Now it seemed they might be important again. If Kathy could find a way to know when she would be left alone for a while, it would be easier to escape.

She began to be interested in what was going on around her, to try and fit it into some kind of pattern. At first the comings and goings of the nursing staff appeared haphazard, and Kathy's hopes for escape seemed futile.

Then Kathy discovered that she could mark time by paying attention to when her meals came. If she had just eaten, a nurse would come in soon after to remove her tray. Sometimes they gave her a bath afterwards, or made her bed. But sometimes, during what she later realized were shift changes, the nurses would leave Kathy alone for a while. She realized that when there were lots of voices and extra noises outside her room that this would be her "private time"–the time of day that Kathy liked best, when she was alone and no one was making demands upon her.

One evening during change of shift, when most of the nurses were off in a cubicle giving their reports, and only one nurse was at the desk, keeping a watchful eye on the monitors, Kathy made her move. Kathy had been so "good" lately that the nurses had begun tying her restraints a little more loosely, giving her extra room to turn over in bed. This time it was going to be an easy job to rid her of their restriction.

Unfettered once again, Kathy nonetheless knew that the hardest part was yet to come. Would she have the strength this time? Slowly, carefully, Kathy edged over the side of her bed, placing first one foot and then the other on the floor. Bracing herself, she stood up, holding onto the bed for support. She took a deep breath. The eating routine had paid off. She felt much stronger. With a guarded look toward the nurse's desk, Kathy began to inch toward the door, bending over like an old lady and shuffling her feet.

Her heart pounded; she faced the most dangerous part. Once out of her room, she had to pass within view of the nurse's desk. Luck was with her! The nurse had her back turned and was talking on the telephone. As her gown flapped open behind her, Kathy shuffled as quickly as she could through the danger zone and out into the hall, where she leaned against the wall, panting.

I'm free! She thought. *I'm getting out of here! Now, how do I go home?* There were so many doors. Which one led to home?

Kathy frantically scanned the row of doorways. She did not know which way to run. Then she glimpsed a tree behind a window in one of the doors. *That must be the way outside,* she thought. Gathering all her energy, Kathy made a rush for the door and, heaving against it, managed to push it open far enough for her to squeeze out.

It was cold. The feel of metal grating beneath her feet made Kathy shiver. There must be some mistake; this was not the right way after all. But she did not know where to go from here. Kathy sat down on the fire escape and began to cry.

"Kathy! Thank God we found you!" An Oriental nurse had opened the door to the fire escape and was worriedly checking Kathy for injuries. Finding none, she relaxed into a scolding. "Kathy! I thought we were done with these little tricks! And just when we were about to take off your restraints, too. Well when the doctor hears about this, I'm afraid he'll say, "No way!"

Kathy began to cry in earnest, great racking sobs that touched the nurse deeply.

"Kathy, it's okay," she soothed, sitting down beside her and bringing Kathy's head onto her lap. "You don't like to be tied down do you? It makes you feel helpless, doesn't it?"

Kathy stopped crying to look up into the nurse's eyes. Here was someone who finally understood. She nodded her head vehemently. *Yes that's it. That's it exactly.* "Okay," said the nurse. "You come with me now. Get back into bed where you belong and *stay there.* Then I'll see what I can do." Kathy struggled to her feet, with the nurse, although smaller than she, lending a strong supportive arm. They

48

walked slowly back into the ICU, where several other nurses were anxiously pacing the floor.

"Oh, thank God, you've found her," said one, as she rushed over to help.

Back once again in her bed, Kathy's eyes pleaded, looking from the restraints into the face of the Oriental nurse. *You promised,* her expression said.

"Stay with her, but don't tie her down," said the nurse. "I'm going to put a call in to Dr. Andrews. I'll be right back."

A few minutes later she returned, smiling. "Well, Kathy–good news," she said. "No more restraints. But you have to promise that there will be no more running away, okay?" She gave Kathy a meaningful look.

Kathy shook her head, *okay.* They had made a pact.

Kathy pushed the game piece aside and turned away. Her head was beginning to throb. She had been concentrating too hard. She had tried to play the game that her mom and Jean had brought for her. What was it they had called it? Scribble? No *Scrabble.* But she just could not seem to get the knack of it. There were little letters, like ABC's. Kathy remembered those. Mom, Beth and Jean expected her to do something with the letters, but Kathy did not know what. It was frustrating and embarrassing. *I should know this,* Kathy said over and over to herself. *If only I could remember.*

She sank back into her pillows. She felt better now that she had been moved out of the ICU unit into a semiprivate room. There was less commotion around her, and it was easier for her if she could focus her attention on just one thing at a time. But this game–she knew they were trying to help, but Kathy felt pressured to perform, and she just was not able to do it. And then she felt as though she had disappointed her family. Maybe she just wasn't trying hard enough. *No, damn it! I am trying!* She thought. *It's just the swelling from the operation. They just need to give me a little more time. It's only temporary. My memory will come back and I will be able to talk again. I know I will. Just give me a little time.*

Kathy felt her mother's eyes on her, and she turned to look at her. *I wish they wouldn't look at me like that,* Kathy thought, *so sad. I hate sadness. I hate this place!*

"Kathy?" Virginia prompted her child, but Kathy did not respond. "It's okay, Kathy. If you don't feel like playing Scrabble, we can try something else. You used to like to play cards. Would you like to play cards?"

No answer.

"I guess not. Maybe you'd like to be alone for a while." Virginia gathered her things and kissed Kathy's cheek. Kathy turned to give her mother a grateful smile. Mother and sister tiptoed out of the room, closing the door behind them. Kathy breathed a sigh of relief.

Well, God, here I am, Kathy thought. *Now what? You sent me back, and here I am. But I don't know what I'm supposed to do. You took my baby away, so I'm not going to be a mother. It's probably just as well; I can't seem to remember things like I used to. What if I forgot to feed the baby? I'm sure you had a good reason, God, but it's still not fair. Bill and the baby and I would have been a family, just like I always wanted. But you took the baby away. You took the baby away.* Kathy sobbed, giving in to the overwhelming sadness that washed over her, threatening to drown her.

When the tears subsided, Kathy soothed herself with an old nursery rhyme. *There was an old woman. She lived in a shoe. She had so many children, she didn't know what to do...* Kathy's mind drifted off to a happier time and place.

℘--------------------൦ര

As they were leaving Kathy's room, Virginia and Jean

ran into Dr. Andrews,

"Oh, Dr. Andrews, I'm glad we caught you," said Virginia, offering her hand. "There are a few things I need to discuss with you. As you know, we're all very grateful for what you've done for Kathy. She's been through a lot, and we're just thankful to have her still with us. But now that her physical problems seem to be under control, we were wondering–what kind of progress can we expect from her mentally?"

"Frankly, I'm a little worried. You and the nurses told us to stimulate her in whatever way we could, talking, reading to her, and playing games. But I'm not sure how much we're getting through. For instance, today we tried to play Scrabble. Scrabble was always one of Kathy's favorite games. But she didn't seem to know what we were doing. She just stared at the letters and then tuned us out. Doctor, please tell me this can't be permanent. We expected that she would have some communication problems and that they would be complicated by the swelling from the operation. But it has been two weeks now. I don't think she's getting any better. This can't be *it*. There must be something more we can do for her. What do we do next?"

"I understand your concern, Mrs. Hughes," Dr. Andrews said. "I am sympathetic to your situation. I know you want to see Kathy improve. But, the truth is, we're in largely uncharted territory. Yes, I do still feel that Kathy will regain more function in the area of communication, both verbal and comprehensive. But it may take some time.

"Right now, Kathy's depressed, and rightly so. She may be shying away from the outside world because of depression, fear, or embarrassment. Her behavior at this point does not unduly concern me.

"But since you are concerned with her future, perhaps a PICA test would give us some answers. Of course, we normally wait a few weeks longer, until the brain swelling has completely subsided, to begin testing."

"What exactly is a PICA test?" asked Jean.

"Well, it's relatively simple," began Dr. Andrews. "The patient is evaluated on her ability to recognize and name a certain number of everyday objects. Sort of a reality testing, to give us a clue as to where the patient stands."

"I want Kathy to have that," Jean stated emphatically.

"Oh, she will, but as I said, it will probably be a few weeks..."

"No, I want her to have it now," Jean interrupted. "I have to know what's going on in Kathy's mind.

"All right," conceded Dr. Andrews. "I'll schedule a PICA test for tomorrow morning."

ℰℴ---------------------ℭℛ

Kathy sat on the side of her bed, a tray of objects laid out in front of her. Jean and Beth were there and so were several doctors. They were all staring at her, waiting.

"Let's try this one again, Kathy," one of them said, pointing to an object. "What is this? What do you do with it?"

Kathy strained to think. The object was familiar. She knew it, but she just could not think of it right now. It was like sometimes before when she would try to say a word and couldn't think of it right away. She would have it on the tip of her tongue, and if she would just wait a few moments, it would come to her. This was the way she felt now. But it was not coming. She had been waiting a long time now. She could feel the people staring at her, wanting her to hurry. *If you'd just give me a little time and not push me,* thought Kathy, *I might get it.* But no, it didn't seem to be coming. Maybe it never would. Kathy turned her head away, embarrassed.

"Kathy," Beth prompted her. "Kathy, remember you used that this morning. You used it to fix your hair. You know what to do with it. Can you tell us?"

No! No! No! Kathy shook her head vehemently and pushed the comb away. She was tired. It seemed that they had been at it for hours, pressuring her, watching her, embarrassing her in front of all these people. Enough was enough. Kathy started to cry.

"Okay, Kathy, that's all for now," the man in charge said. "Ms. Hughes, I'm afraid we won't get any more out of her now."

They left Kathy alone; Jean followed the herd of onlookers out the door. She stopped the speech pathologist, grabbing his coat sleeve, as he was about to get away.

"Wait," she said. "Tell me what this means."

"I'll give you a full report as soon as I evaluate all the data and look over Kathy's chart," he said. "But right now it doesn't look good. You saw her. She didn't know what a comb was, or a matchbook or a pencil. Twelve everyday objects and she could name maybe three.

"We'll be retesting her, of course. As Dr. Andrews explained to you, we normally give this test four weeks after surgery. At that time we can expect the results to be a fairly accurate prediction of what the patient's recovery will be six months down the road. Since it's only been two weeks for Kathy, her poor performance may have something to do with the swelling. Let's hope so. But if these problems understanding language that we saw exhibited here today persist, her prognosis is very, very poor. Right now, I'd say there's not much hope for her ever to return to a normal life."

Jean gasped.

"I'm sorry, Ms. Hughes, but you asked."

The group of doctors retreated, a curtain of white fading into the background, as tears filled Jean's eyes.

Chapter 7

A STRANGE NEW LIFE

Life on the regular ward was better, Kathy decided. Hospitals were for sick people, and Kathy still did not like this one, but at least now she had more privacy, more time to herself. *I'm becoming a loner,* thought Kathy. *That's strange for me. I always liked parties, fun, wild and crazy friends. Now I like to be alone.*

I'm glad my roommate is quiet, too, thought Kathy. *Jean and Beth said they were sorry I had to get an old lady for a roommate, but I'm not sorry. She's nice. She's quiet. We get along fine.*

Kathy dozed off but was soon awakened by the sound of moaning. At first she thought it must be her own troubled dreams, but then she remembered she was not alone. The sounds were coming from the next bed. The nice old lady was in pain. Kathy sat up, wanting to call out to the lady and reassure her, but she knew it would be useless. The lady would not understand.

Feeling helpless, Kathy looked over at her roommate and gave her a reassuring smile. *It's okay,* she wanted to say. *I know how you feel. It will get better.* But the old lady did not get better. She continued to moan and then to gasp. Kathy became frightened. *Something is really wrong,* she thought. *Where are the nurses?*

Suddenly, with great effort, the old woman spoke. It was only a whisper, and Kathy had to strain to make it out. "Help me. Call the nurse. Help me, please," she begged.

Kathy was panic-stricken. *Oh my God,* she thought. *I've got to do something. The lady needs help. I have to get the nurses to come help the lady. But how?*

Kathy's mind whirled. She had not been told how to use the call button. They had figured that it would be a waste of time to teach someone who can't communicate to use a call button.

There was only one way. Kathy had no choice. If the nurses would not come to her, she had to go to them. She forgot about the failure of her previous attempts at walking alone. She had been to physical therapy since then. Although her right leg was still dragging, Kathy made good progress with the therapist at her side. She could do it alone. She had to. The lady needed a nurse, and Kathy had no choice but to get her one.

Carefully getting out of bed, Kathy remembered to use her good leg to support herself while she maneuvered her right leg into position. Besides the dragging leg, her right hand was almost useless, and Kathy had to lean heavily on her left hand, using all her strength to push herself up. Still it was easier than the last time she had done it alone. *Practice makes perfect,* Kathy thought wryly.

Walking was also easier this time, and once up, Kathy quickly made it to the door She gave the lady a hopeful look, trying to communicate, "Hang on, I'll be right back." She knew she had to go down the left hallway to find the nurses' desk. They always took that route when she had physical therapy. Determination and the feeling of finally doing something useful gave Kathy the confidence to forge ahead. It was not easy. She knew she was taking a risk. Once she got to the nurses' station, they might think she was running away again. They might not understand that she was trying to help. Somehow she had to make them understand.

She saw the nurses' desk. There were three nurses there, two writing in charts, and one talking on the phone. None of the three looked her way. She was getting tired when she shuffled up to the desk and finally was noticed.

"Kathy, what are you doing?" a nurse scolded her. "How many times must we tell you..." Kathy shook her head vehemently. *Wait. Please listen,* she tried to say with a pleading look.

"Just a minute," another nurse interrupted. "Kathy is

something wrong?" Kathy nodded yes.

"Come," Kathy stammered. "Come...here." She turned her head in the direction of her room.

"She wants us to go to her room," the nurse said, understanding Kathy's urgent message. "Let's go."

Two nurses quickly walked to Kathy's room while the third, helping Kathy, trailed behind. By the time Kathy and her nurse had reached the room, one of the other two was running back out the door.

"It's Mrs. Johnson," she said as she raced by. "Get the emergency cart. I'm calling Dr. Boland, stat."

Kathy was a heroine. Mrs. Johnson had been rushed off to surgery, and Kathy's quick actions had played an important role in her recovery. When Dr. Andrews was informed of Kathy's direct and articulate message, he was very impressed. Perhaps they had been too quick to judge Kathy. Suddenly she went from being looked upon as a lost cause to "having potential."

Kathy basked in the positive attention, her self esteem bolstered by finally having something to be proud of. She smiled to herself and thought, *See, I knew I could do it. And now they know it, too.*

Several days later, Dr. Andrews walked into Kathy's room. "Kathy," he said. "I've got good news. You're going home."

Kathy sat bolt upright. Her eyes grew wide and tears rimmed them. Home–home to her little cottage, home to her work, home to Bill–finally, she was going home.

Kathy heard little else of what the doctor said. Something about therapy. Yes, she could see that it would be wise to continue some type of therapy for a while. That was okay. The main thing was that she was going home.

Riding down in the wheelchair the next morning, Kathy was met by well-wishing nurses and hospital personnel all along the route from her room to the emergency entrance where her brother, Rich, and sister, Jean, were picking her up.

"Good luck, Kathy," they all said as she wheeled by. "She'll need it," someone muttered not quite under her breath.

Kathy smiled and waved, feeling like a beauty queen in a parade. *Hospitals are more fun to leave than to stay in,* she decided.

When Rich had pulled the car around, he came over to help Kathy into the passenger's seat. In his hand he carried a football helmet. Kathy thought it was a joke, to lift her spirits. *That's cute but it's not necessary,* she thought. *My spirits are soaring just because I'm going home.* But when Rich looked at Kathy, his face was serious.

"Kathy you have to wear this. It's Dr. Andrews's orders. We have to protect the area of your brain where the skull is missing. If I stopped quickly or had an accident, your brain could be hurt again–hurt bad. Do you understand?"

Kathy thought about it for a moment. She had not looked at herself very much in the hospital. She had forgotten about the area of her skull that was dented in and flattened. Oh, what the heck–as long as she was going home, who cared? Helmet or no helmet, it didn't matter. She nodded her assent.

Relieved to have gotten through this initial barrier so easily, Rich sighed and smiled at Kathy. "You're being super, Kathy," he said. He strapped the helmet onto Kathy's head and helped her into the car.

They drove for a while, then parked and got out. Kathy was not paying much attention. The places Kathy saw out of the car window as they zipped along had a slightly familiar, yet far away quality. Kathy assumed it was because she was still not near enough to her home for her to easily recognize landmarks. At any rate, she was glad they were taking a break. Maybe they would get a snack, too. She was beginning to get her appetite back and was feeling hungry now.

Kathy followed Rich and Jean inside a building. People

were milling about. Some had suitcases, but this did not strike Kathy as strange at first. Then she saw Bill! He had come to meet her, to take her the rest of the way home! Oh, dear, sweet Bill. How thoughtful. How she loved him!

Bill approached Kathy slowly, almost reluctantly. *He doesn't know what to say,* thought Kathy. *For once, Bill is at a loss for words.* But Kathy didn't need words. She walked over to him and laid her head on his shoulder.

"Well, Kathy." Rich broke in. "We'd better get going. We have a plane waiting."

A plane! Of course! This was an airport. Jean and Rich must be going back to St. Louis. Kathy hugged Bill tightly for a moment then, putting her hand in his, followed after Rich and Jean.

When they got to the gate, Rich gave Jean a worried look. Jean took a deep breath, then faced her sister.

"Kathy, we're going home," she said, "You and me. Home to St. Louis."

Kathy's face dropped. Her mind reeled. She stared at Jean in disbelief. What did she mean—the two of them! Oh, no! No Way! Jean was going to St. Louis. That was her home, not Kathy's. Port Clinton was home for Kathy. Kathy was going to Port Clinton—with Bill. She looked at Bill for confirmation. He was staring at the floor.

What's going on? Kathy struggled to understand and was beginning to get angry. *Who do they think they are to decide where I should go? I have to get back to work. I have things to do. 1 can go to St. Louis another time. But not now. Now I have to get home.*

"Kathy," Jean started to explain. "Kathy, you're not able to take care of yourself. You need to go home so Mom and Dad and all of the family can help you."

I don't need your help! Kathy thought, outraged. Her independent streak had been triggered, and Kathy was not about to be dictated to. "No!" she said, pulling away from Bill, from all of them.

"Be reasonable," Rich pleaded. "We already have the

tickets. See?" Jean produced the tickets as proof.

"Kathy," Rich continued. "I know you wanted to go back to Port Clinton, but it's just not possible now." He put his arm around Kathy, but she pulled away.

Mean! She thought. *You're mean. All of you! You tried to trick me, but I won't do it. I won't go to St. Louis! I won't!* Kathy looked pleadingly at Jean, who more than anyone else could understand her thoughts. *Please, Jean,* her eyes begged.

Jean looked at Kathy. She knew that stance; it was a stand off. To get Kathy on that plane, she knew they would have to drag her bodily, kicking and screaming all the way. So, now what?

"Let me call Dr. Andrews," said Jean. "Maybe he can convince her to go." Jean left to find a phone booth.

When she came back, Jean reported. "Dr. Andrews said that if she refused to go to St. Louis not to force her. He suggested we go to Port Clinton for the weekend, then go to St. Louis on Monday. I think he has a good idea. What do you say?"

"Okay by me," said Rich. "You know how stubborn Kathy is. I don't think we could get her on the plane right now without a straight jacket."

Kathy picked up little of their conversation, but she sensed she had gotten her way. Jean turned to her. "Kathy, you win, we're going to Port Clinton. But first we have to call Mom."

Kathy smiled. "Okay, dokey," she said.

Virginia was choosing her words carefully as she spoke long distance to Kathy. Jean had called her from the airport and told her of their change of plans. She must somehow make sure that Kathy would not refuse to get on the plane again on Monday. She had to convince Kathy to cooperate with them. It was the only way. She knew Kathy understood more than they gave her credit for; if she spoke slowly and simply, she could get through to Kathy.

"Kathy," Virginia continued. "I have made plans for

you to go to therapy. Dr. Andrews said you need therapy. Remember? Well, I have it all set up. Everyone is expecting you. We all have worked hard to get you the help you need. Please help us help you. Promise me you will come home Monday with Jean. Promise *me*."

Kathy vacillated. It was hard to say no to her mother. They all wanted to help her. She began to feel guilty. Maybe she could go back to St. Louis for just a while. Maybe a month at the most. "0-k-kay," she stammered. *"I'll do it for you, Mom. But only for a month—no longer."*

₠--------------------ℂ

Kathy's heart leaped for joy at the sight of her little cottage on the lake. This was home—her home, her friends, her life. All of it revolved around this little strip of land on Sandpiper Court. Oh, did it feel good to be back. It was as if she had never been gone. All of her possessions were waiting for her: the jukebox where she played all the old songs that brought fond memories—the crazy college days, the wild life of the French Quarter in New Orleans—, her TV, which kept her company on the nights when Bill did not come around. Wistfully, Kathy went from room to room, touching objects. Each one was a memory, a link to the life she loved.

Jean helped Kathy unpack and fixed them all sandwiches for dinner. Kathy was content just to be at home, but the others seemed self-conscious.

Unsure about what to do next, Bill suggested, "Kathy, why don't we invite some of your close friends over? They have all been asking about you and are anxious to see you."

Kathy was not feeling like having company. But she hated to say no to Bill. And she did not want to be rude to her friends. *Okay*, she nodded, and her friends were called.

It was a disaster. The noise and confusion of everyone talking at once was more than Kathy could handle. She tried to talk, but could not. She cursed, even though she did not mean to.

"That's the spirit, Kathy," her friends said. But they were wrong. It was not what she wanted to do. Then she tried singing. She had found at the hospital that for some reason singing came more easily to her. So she tried to say what she wanted by singing the words. But she could not carry a tune, and she felt embarrassed. She soon gave up the effort.

Bill came to her rescue. He could see that Kathy was bewildered and her capacities were being over-taxed. He brought her some medication that the doctor had prescribed.

"Here, Kathy, it's time for your pill," Bill said, placing it in the palm of her hand. "Take this and I'll help you to bed. Everyone will understand. It's been a long day, your first day home, and you need to rest."

Kathy didn't like pills. She rarely took them, even aspirin, and she hated the thought of taking a prescription drug. Pills made her feel out of control. She liked to run her own life, and that included taking care of her own body. But Bill was waiting, and Kathy realized she had little choice. She took the pill.

As she drifted off into a drugged sleep, Kathy vowed, *They may be able to tell me what to do now, but not for long–not for long.*

The next day was Saturday, and Kathy and Jean took a walk into town to go to the post office. Kathy drank in the fresh air, the sunshine, and the smell of the lake. She felt renewed. She was at peace. After the long weeks of confinement, she relished the familiar sensations.

When they got to the post office, Kathy wanted to check her mail. She always did this every day, without fail. She did not mind having to go downtown to get her mail. It helped create some of the small town atmosphere that she loved. Here in Port Clinton, everyone knew everyone else. They often milled about downtown around the post office, exchanging bits of gossip. It was a homey and friendly sort of town, and the influx of tourists in the summer season suited Kathy as well. The tourists added excitement and pizzazz.

Jean had to help Kathy find her box. Kathy could not remember where it was. Once they found it, they discovered that it had been closed.

"Oh, I forgot," Jean said apologetically. "We had your mail forwarded to St. Louis. We didn't think you'd be coming back here."

Kathy was furious. *How dare you,* she thought. *This is my personal property. My private stuff. How dare you send it somewhere without asking me.* She glared at Jean, her feelings of betrayal and anger clearly communicated.

Jean bowed her head. She understood her sister's helpless frustration. "I'm sorry, Kathy," she repeated.

Silently they walked back to Kathy's apartment.

That night there was a party. Some of Kathy's friends were getting together. It was just an informal affair. Did Kathy want to go? Of course, if Bill was going, Kathy would go, too.

At the party Kathy got her first real taste of her new reality. It was like a slap in the face. People were milling around her, talking, laughing, drinking, and having fun—doing the things she used to do. But to Kathy the activity seemed distant, out of focus. There were too many things going on, like a kaleidoscope that was churning too fast.

She knew she could not talk well. So she decided to just listen to her friends' conversations. Just being with them would be enough. But what Kathy had not expected was the embarrassed look on her friends' faces when they talked to her. They were uncomfortable around her. They didn't know how to react to her new condition. Some were clearly shocked.

Kathy felt isolated. She was no longer part of the gang. She was a misfit. Her own friends could not accept her. Was she really that bad? She did not seem so to herself, but clearly Kathy's friends saw her differently. Perhaps it was not a bad idea after all to go to St. Louis. Once she had received therapy and could talk again, her friends would not feel uncomfortable around her. Then she could get on with her life.

Okay, she thought. It will only be a month or so anyway. I'll go.

Chapter 8

THE STRUGGLE UPWARD

Kathy stood, plate in hand, near the kitchen counter and gave her Mom a bewildered look. Virginia, accustomed now to her daughter's wide-eyed stares, put down the dish she was wiping and walked over to Kathy.

She repeated her instruction–"Kathy, put the plate on the table."

Kathy did not move.

Virginia sighed. Had it only been a week? It seemed like forever since Kathy had returned home. She glanced into the dining room where several deflated balloons still hung by bits of tape to the wall, remnants of Kathy's welcome home party. Oh, she was grateful to have Kathy home. Virginia, a devout Catholic, never failed to thank God every day for her daughter's recovery. But the worst was not over yet.

In many ways it was like having another baby. Virginia felt she had hardly had time to breathe a sigh of relief. After nearly two decades of childrearing, she was finally at the point of having some time alone, when her youngest daughter, Laura, entered kindergarten next month. But now, with Kathy home, there was more work than ever.

She thought that in many ways it was worse than having a baby. With a baby, you did not expect much. There were fewer disappointments. With Kathy, Virginia often found herself getting frustrated when she would momentarily forget about Kathy's limitations. It made it all the more painful to watch when she was reminded that her daughter was not and never would be the same. She sighed again. She was a patient person. She would handle this. Anyway, what choice did she have?

Wiping her hands on her apron, Virginia looked

directly into her daughter's eyes and said once more, "Kathy, put the *plate* on the *table.*" As she spoke, Virginia took Kathy's limp right hand in hers and placed it first on the plate Kathy was holding, and then, walking a few steps, onto the kitchen table. "This is a plate," she said. "This is a table. We put the plate *on* the table." Virginia guided Kathy's hand until finally the deed was done.

At times like this she wanted to cry. Raising twelve kids had been no picnic. But she had loved it all—the hard work, the cramped living quarters. The big old house had been added on to so many times it was hard to remember just how small it had started out. And through it all, her deep family commitment and her faith in God had made Virginia strong. She was devoted to her family and would do anything for them—even this, even now, when it was supposed to be *her* time, her turn to relax and enjoy life. Even now, she would put that aside and devote herself to helping her daughter. Kathy had to be taught all over again. Like a child, she had to be led step by step through the difficult process of reorganizing her brain.

Virginia thought back to that first meeting at the rehabilitation center just five days earlier. She had taken Kathy to St. John's Hospital in St. Louis, where Kathy had been on the social services staff several years before. It had been hard, harder it seemed on those who knew Kathy before than even on Kathy herself. Kathy was still not fully aware of the dramatic change in herself, but to her friends, it was painfully evident. There had been a reunion of sorts. Several of Kathy's former co-workers had come down to wish her well. They had obviously been taken aback by the change in her appearance and her demeanor. Kathy had had the reputation of being the most fun—loving member of their group. Always ready for a party, Kathy would change her plans on the spur of the moment if an opportunity came up. She made them laugh. She lifted their spirits with her humor and good nature and she could always be counted on to point out the positive side of a situation. To Kathy, life was for living–moment by moment–taking all that was good and ignoring the rest.

So it was quite a shock to see Kathy subdued, so quiet and unresponsive. Not only that, Kathy's physical appearance reflected her trauma as well. She wore a scarf to hide her dented head, but it was evident nonetheless, as was the shaved area on Kathy's otherwise full head of hair. She looked like a defeated individual for whom life was a drudgery to be endured at best. Little did they know of Kathy's inner struggle, of her shame and anger at being put in this embarrassing situation. Kathy loved her friends. She wanted their support, not their pity. Unfortunately, she was a pitiful sight to behold.

Then there were the tests. Tests would become a way of life for Kathy. Tests to evaluate her abilities, to measure her performance against "normal" standards. Kathy would be labeled and categorized many times over in the years to come, but would never really be understood. For the tests could only evaluate her outward performance, not her inner perceptions and understanding. This inner life was to prove frustrating to Kathy, as over and over she had to deal with the fact that she knew more than she could express, that she was more than the sum total of her test scores. For some patients, this difference was the ultimate slap in the face, the hurdle they could not overcome. For those with less determination and willful stubbornness than Kathy, who were labeled of "dull" intelligence and considered unable to voice an intelligible protest, it could mark the beginning of the end. They would become complacent in the face of hopelessness and allow their families to "take them home and make them comfortable," as Kathy's parents had been urged to do.

But Kathy was not an average person. And her mother knew that. In spite of indecisive doctors, who could not seem to agree on a prognosis or offer a standard for therapy, Virginia was determined to give Kathy every opportunity to recover as much of her capacities as possible. She believed that Kathy needed to start some kind, any kind of therapy, *right away*. She had managed to enroll Kathy into therapy at St. John's Hospital partly because her husband was a staff physician there, even though at that time they had no organized therapy for head trauma victims.

Because they did not know what else to do with her, they treated Kathy like a stroke victim, for her condition did have much in common with the effects of a stroke. Although Kathy's problems came from physical damage to the brain tissue itself, the end result was much the same as a patient whose brain tissue had been damaged by lack of oxygen during a stroke. Both incidents cause irreparable damage to nerve and brain tissue, resulting in a loss of ability in the activities governed by the part of the brain that had been damaged.

Kathy's condition resembled a stroke to the left side of the brain, which affected the language center of the brain. Both her sensory input and output nerve centers were impaired, making it difficult for Kathy to process the information she received and to communicate her thoughts in language. The basic knowledge was still there, but putting it into words was now almost impossible. That explained why Kathy knew what to *do* with a comb, but did not know *what* the comb was. She had no words to express what she instinctively understood. Not only that, Kathy's motor skills for language—the memory of how to hold her mouth or move her tongue to make certain sounds—was also affected, though to a lesser degree than in many stroke patients. All in all, much of the memory Kathy needed in order to use language—the names of objects, the ability to remember the words in a sentence long enough to process their meaning, the physical mechanics of speaking the words—all this had been lost, erased when Kathy's head smashed into the sidewalk on the night of the accident.

The doctor explained this situation to Virginia that first day, trying to help her understand Kathy's limitations. They would, of course, do what they could to help Kathy regain as much function as possible, but from their experiences with stroke patients, they thought that a full recovery was extremely unlikely. Yet they said that Kathy was young and who knows, she might do better than they expected.

With this small encouragement, Kathy was put through her first battery of tests. There were intelligence tests, visual and auditory comprehension tests, logic and problem solving tests, and word recognition tests. Kathy had difficulty in all areas, but her worst problems were a direct result of her language deficiencies. The more complex the verbal instructions, the worse she performed. Although Kathy showed a definite ability to comprehend the heart of the matter, giving a specific answer to a specific question was many times beyond her abilities. And it quickly became evident that Kathy also had a memory problem. When an object was laid in front of her, she would occasionally be able to come up with a name for it, although more often than not she either misnamed the object or mispronounced the name. If the object was removed from her field of vision, however, Kathy had no memory whatsoever of having seen it. This problem would prove to have far-reaching implications for Kathy for many years to come, as she would have to relearn the same information over and over before it would finally become imprinted in her brain as a retrievable memory. Only through constant repetition and diligent work would Kathy be able to gain back some of what she lost.

Virginia contemplated all these things and reminded herself to be patient with Kathy. Repetition, they had said, repetition.

Once again Virginia took Kathy's hand. "This is a plate."

For nine months, from late August 1979 to May 1980, Kathy went to therapy as an outpatient at St. John's. Virginia would drive Kathy to the hospital in the morning and pick her up late in the afternoon. Kathy received physical therapy for her physical problems–a slight dragging of her right leg that produced an off balance stride, and the partial paralysis of her right hand. She also went to occupational therapy but concentrated on relearning skills that would help her in everyday life. Kathy worked for hours, practicing using a fork or spoon. Early on, Kathy was forced to make decisions about how she would tackle certain problems. The therapist called it "learning strategies," and this decision process was to become an increasingly important part of Kathy's life.

Kathy's first major strategy decision had far-reaching effects. She was given a choice. She could either spend the majority of her time and effort during occupational therapy working to regain the capacity of her damaged right hand or she could learn to use her left hand as the dominant one, becoming, in effect, left-handed. Kathy chose the latter strategy, demonstrating an unusual acceptance of her situation. She had a fierce determination to achieve her major goal–to learn to talk again. Communication with those around her became Kathy's first priority. She would live with the other problems if she could only communicate again. In making this decision, Kathy exhibited a mature acceptance of her condition and a lack of what the therapist often called "tunnel vision." Many patients were hampered in their recovery by this tunnel vision. If they could not regain their capabilities *just the same* as they were before, many patients would feel defeated and give up. But Kathy, knowing that she had only a limited amount of energy to devote to therapy, chose to become left-handed. In the long run it would prove easier than trying to rehabilitate the paralyzed right hand, which may or may not respond to therapy.

So Kathy's main interest, her obsession, was with speech therapy. Through speech therapy she could learn to talk again. Kathy threw herself into therapy as only one who is driven could do. She sat for long hours in a small, square cubicle that held only a table and two chairs. Sitting across the table from her speech therapist, Kathy doggedly worked through page after page of work sheets. She had been assigned to a young speech therapist, a girl who had just finished her training. All the other speech therapists had known Kathy prior to the accident, and they did not feel they could work with Kathy. It would be too hard, too embarrassing and painful for both Kathy and the therapists. Kathy needed from the start to rebuild her self-confidence, her belief in herself. She had to create a new image of herself as confident and capable within the new limits of her existence. Having a constant reminder of the life she left behind could only hinder the effort to rebuild her life. She must look to the future, not to the past.

And if the work was challenging to Kathy it was equally challenging to Susan, her therapist. Susan had never worked with a head injury victim before; she and Kathy were learning together. In some ways, more experience might have helped Susan; but on the other hand, Susan's expectations of Kathy were not limited by previous experiences. She simply started where Kathy was and hoped to gain as much ground as possible, always with the goal of moving Kathy forward, progressing, however slowly to the next step.

And the work was slow. Speech therapy is by nature a painfully slow process, requiring great patience on the part of both the therapist and the patient. Before the accident, Kathy was never known for her patience, but after, as happens to many head injury patients, Kathy became more focused; she developed a "one track mind." On the positive side, this helped Kathy to stick to a task long past the point where she became bored or tired of it. But most of all it was determination that kept Kathy working.

At first the work was mostly picture identification. Susan would show Kathy a picture of an object and ask Kathy to identify it. In the beginning Kathy was wrong most of the time. But after long hours of repetition and gentle reminders from Susan, Kathy began to remember again. This was a cup. This was a table. This was a girl. On and on it went, gently coaxing Kathy's brain to reorganize, to remember again, to speak again.

"C-c-c-u-up." Kathy worked painstakingly on pronunciation, willing her mind and mouth to cooperate. At first Kathy could not remember her body parts or their functions. The early months were spent in intensive work on the basics.

At home, Virginia took over where the therapist left off. "Eggs, Kathy, toast, milk, cereal," over and over Virginia repeated and Kathy listened, slowly, slowly remembering, then painfully trying to repeat the words she heard. Sometimes Kathy lost her enthusiasm. It was so hard, the work so slow. At times like that, Kathy would break down and cry. Often Virginia cried with her. "Why me? Why us?" they asked. God, if he was listening, did not answer.

Kathy, so free and friendly before, now became a loner. She retreated from family and friends, partly from embarrassment, partly for the sake of survival. After the accident, Kathy's mind could not discriminate between background noise and conversation. Consequently, if the television was playing in the background when someone spoke to Kathy, she could not filter out the noise of the TV and concentrate on the words being spoken to her. Both noises clamored equally for her attention. As a result, Kathy was unable to understand either of them. She found out early that in order to understand what was being said to her, she had to give it her undivided attention. In a quiet room, on a one to one basis, this worked quite well, and Kathy's speech improved, as did her comprehension. But in a normal, busy household such as Virginia's, Kathy was overwhelmed. Gradually her family adapted to her need for solitude and gave her plenty of time alone. Kathy and her mom became closer, bound together by their common goal and by the unprecedented amount of time they spent together.

Virginia often worried about Kathy. She had indeed been the rebel of the family. Running off by herself, living alone in strange cities, Kathy's uncritical acceptance of people and her lack of fear had always worried Virginia. Now Virginia worried about Kathy for different reasons. Could she accept this drastic change in her life style, the limitations, her dependency on others? Could she move beyond it and regain control of her life? If so, how much responsibility could Kathy handle?

So much was unknown, just questions without answers. Virginia was torn between protecting her child and pushing her to the limits of her abilities. Not yet knowing what these limits were, Virginia feared for Kathy's eventual peace of mind. She knew Kathy would never be content with less than full independence, yet that goal seemed an impossible dream.

Virginia need not have worried. Although Kathy was depressed and cried a lot during those first months, she never gave up. That, above all else, seemed to be the key to Kathy's eventual success. Kathy had faith—faith that she was spared for a reason, faith that she was meant to lead a meaningful life. Kathy knew God had told her to come back. She did not know why yet, but she felt a deep commitment to fulfill her life's purpose, whatever that would be. Besides, hadn't Bill said to her, "Get well Kathy. Just get well."

Life at home with Virginia and Laura seemed to meet Kathy's needs at the time perfectly well. Kathy had more of Virginia's patient attention than ever before. Virginia was a committed teacher—she was the mother of the student. As only a mother can do, Virginia gave Kathy instructions and confidence, understanding and self-discipline. Friends, even while keeping their distance out of respect for Kathy's wishes, wanted to help also. Laura's kindergarten teacher sent home extra copies of Laura's books and worksheets. Together Kathy and Laura learned their ABC's. Laura progressed faster than Kathy, but Kathy did not mind. She was happy just to be learning again.

One of Kathy's closest friends, Maggie, was a Montessori teacher for preschool children. When she learned about Kathy's language difficulties, Maggie immediately wanted to help. She had learned patience through her work with small children, and she loved to teach. So several evenings each week, Maggie would come to Virginia's house and work with Kathy. They started with phonics, concentrating on Kathy's reading problems. Kathy relearned how to put sounds together to make words. She moved from the ABC's to simple words. It was slow. Maggie would show Kathy a picture of an object, and then she would write the name of the object in Kathy's workbook as she read it out loud. She would show Kathy the picture again and have Kathy copy the word beside the picture. Kathy would copy the word fifty times or more as she looked at the picture and repeated the word to herself. Slowly, Kathy learned to associate the picture, the sound, the letters, and the word. So many steps to remembering a simple word like cat, dog, or cup. It was tedious work, but Kathy kept at it.

By Christmas of 1979, Kathy was speaking well enough to be understood. She often used the wrong verb tense, and prepositions and pronouns were especially difficult for her. Kathy would say 'she' for 'he,' 'it' for 'them,' 'up' for 'down.' But those closest to Kathy, her family and friends, knew what she meant. On top of everything else, Kathy had to relearn grammar and sentence structure. But however scrambled, Kathy was getting her message across. It was a start. She was communicating. The door that had shut so tightly separating Kathy from the rest of society was opening just a crack.

Kathy had little contact with Bill during this time. He called a few times, but since Kathy could not talk well, phone conversations were difficult. Bill did most of the talking, and the conversations were strained.

"Kathy! How's it going?"

"Okay." (Kathy was not a complainer.)

"Well, I've been busy-construction jobs, friends, all that... Well, uh, I hope things are going well... I'll call you later..."

Bill sounded distant, out of touch, but Kathy had other things on her mind. Worry began to needle at her, however. Bill was not fond of being alone, and he was so handsome and charming. All the girls liked him. Kathy decided she had to go back to Port Clinton, to Bill–just a short visit, to reassure herself.

The family was against the trip, but Kathy stood her ground. She had given up her cottage, they argued. There was no need to go back. She should just stay put and concentrate on her therapy. Still Kathy was adamant. Yes, she had given up her cottage, and it had broken her heart. When she started therapy, Kathy knew deep inside that it was going to be a long haul. But Port Clinton was still her home. She had ties there. She had Bill.

"Kathy, how would you manage?" her mother asked, worried about the plane ride, the airport, and the logistics of the whole thing. It was only a fifty-five minute trip, and under normal circumstances it would be no problem. But for Kathy...

"I'm okay," said Kathy, knowing full well she was not.

"Well, she would be met at the airport," Jean finally suggested. "It wouldn't be like she would have to find her own way. Bill would be picking her up. What could go wrong?"

Finally they gave in, knowing Kathy would do it on her own if they did not help. They got it all lined up–the round-trip ticket, the arrangements–and wrote Kathy a chart, showing in large print the time and place she was to meet Bill. Everything seemed in order, and Kathy boarded the plane without incident. She knew her instructions–stay put until the plane arrives at its final destination.

Kathy was nervous, a little scared. It was her first venture alone since the accident. Had she not been so determined to see Bill, to check on him, she would not have dared to do this. Somewhere in the debris of the accident, a bit of Kathy's adventurous spirit had been lost. Right now she would much rather be safe at home at her mother's house instead of unsure and self-conscious out on her own.

Kathy breathed a sigh of relief, as the stewardess showed her to her seat and helped her fasten the seatbelt. Her obvious physical disability did bring some advantages, she thought. She had gotten the help she needed without having to ask. She settled down in her seat and waited for the plane to take off. Her thoughts naturally turned to Bill. Wouldn't he be happy to see her? *We've been apart too long*, she thought.

The flight was short, one hour, and soon Kathy found herself following the other passengers down the gangplank as they exited the plane.

She frantically searched the crowd for Bill. What if he wasn't there? She had been let down before by Bill's lack of punctuality. He seemed to have a sense of time all his own. She thought back to the nights she had been stood up, waiting alone at her cottage while Bill was at the bar drinking beer and playing pool with his friends. It made her furious, and each time, she swore she would not let him get away with it again. But when he finally showed up with his sheepish grin and little-boy look, her heart melted all over again. Could he help it if he lost track of time? He had not forgotten her, he was just having so much fun... He wouldn't dare do that to her this time, would he? Oh dear, perhaps she should have had someone else meet her. Kathy began to worry. What if he didn't show up? What would she do?

Suddenly she felt an arm around her waist, coming from behind her. She turned. It was Bill! She melted into his arms.

Her three-day weekend was wonderful. Bill was attentive, by her side every moment. He took her to a meeting with a lawyer to discuss the accident. He stepped in when Kathy could not find words to express herself. He buffered her from the world, protecting her, allowing her to experience only as much as she could handle. He was, for once, everything that Kathy had ever wanted him to be— friend, lover, her protector. Kathy was in heaven.

It ended all too soon. Kathy's brother, Rich, arrived in Port Clinton to pick Kathy up and take her to Cleveland, where she would catch her flight home. Kathy cried and clung to Bill, but Bill would not give in. She had to go back. There was much work for her to do.

Reluctantly, Kathy said her last farewell and let go of Bill. They were late, and Rich sped all the way to Cleveland. Even still, they almost missed the flight, and Rich had to shuffle Kathy into the hands of the waiting stewardess, with little explanation. They were the last ones to board the plane.

Settling down in her seat by the window, Kathy closed her eyes and tried to relax. She felt good. Her trip had gone well. She was once again confident of Bill's love. Relieved and happy, Kathy looked forward to completing this last leg of her journey. She missed her family, and she wanted to get back to therapy. Therapy was her work for now, and Kathy wanted to get on with it. Like Bill had said, she had much work to do. And only by working hard could she regain control of her life. Kathy was determined to do just that. Not for a moment did she ever doubt that she would be independent again.

Kathy was startled out of her thoughts by the sound of a child's protesting voice.

"But I wanted to sit at the window," the boy whined. He looked to be about five-years-old.

"Shh," scolded the woman who was sitting in the seat next to Kathy.

"W... w... winder.. ?" questioned Kathy, motioning to the window and then to the boy.

"Yea, yeah!" He squealed in delight.

"If you're sure," started the woman, uncertainty in her voice. She gave Kathy a quizzical look, not sure what to make of her.

"Okay," Kathy nodded, smiling.

The plump woman relaxed her grip on the boy and smiled back at Kathy. "Well, thank you. It's his first trip, you know. He's so excited. Are you going all the way to St. Louis?"

"Yes," Kathy answered, as she began struggling with her seat belt, trying to unsnap it.

"Oh, here, let me help you," offered the woman, noticing Kathy's difficulty. She saw that Kathy was using only one hand.

Kathy sensed the woman examining her, and she wanted to explain herself to make the woman understand, without pitying her, but since she had no words with which to explain, she said nothing. Once free of the seatbelt, Kathy moved over to the opposite aisle seat, giving the boy and his mother the two seats together.

The sound of the pilot's voice came over the intercom, giving notice of takeoff. They were on their way. Not ten minutes later, the pilot came over the intercom again.

"I'm sorry, folks," he announced. "There's a slight malfunction with one of our instruments. There's absolutely nothing to be concerned about, but I'm afraid we will need to get back on the ground and check it out. We will be landing at Dayton Airport. There you will be put on another plane. That flight will be going to Louisville; at Louisville you will be boarded onto a flight to St. Louis. You can expect a delay of several hours from your original arrival time. We apologize for the delay. Again, please rest assured you're in no danger. We will be landing in a few minutes. Please fasten your seatbelts. Thank you."

Kathy panicked. The pilot's words–malfunction... landing... Louisville–were scrambling around in her mind. Intuitively, she knew what it meant. She had flown enough before the accident to piece together the idea that there was a problem and they would be landing at a strange airport. Now what would she do? She was alone and unable to communicate. She did not know where to go. How would she ever get home? Suddenly the whole trip seemed like a bad idea. Kathy started to cry.

"What's wrong?" asked the lady next to Kathy. "You're

not worried are you? The pilot said the plane was okay. It's just a minor malfunction. We'll be safe on the ground very soon."

"No, no, it isn't that." Kathy shook her head, trying to make the lady understand. Her fears were not about the plane. Her fears were deeper. More personal. She tried to put them into words.

"I can't talk... ac-ci-dent... help me?..."

Understanding sparked in the eyes of the woman. *So that's it–brain damage. My God, why have they let her travel alone?*

"Of course," she consoled Kathy, taking her limp hand in one of her plump ones. "You just stay with me. I'll see that you get on the right plane. You said you were going all the way to St. Louis, right?"

Kathy nodded.

"Well, wonderful!" the lady exclaimed. "So are we. You'll just stay with us all the way. We'll be a threesome. Don't worry a bit, honey. I'll see to it that you get home safe and sound."

Kathy stopped sniffling and wiped her eyes. She gave the lady a shy smile.

"Thank her," she said.

"Don't mention it," said the lady, noticing Kathy's error but thinking nothing of it.

When the plane had landed safely, Kathy, her plump rescuer, and her young son walked hand in hand down the concourse to meet their connecting flight.

Settling down into her seat on the second plane, Kathy felt safe. The lady was her friend. She had helped her. She trusted the lady. Suddenly Kathy heard her name being called. "Is Kathy Hughes here?"

A pilot and two stewardesses were walking toward her. Nervously, she raised her hand. What could they want with her?

"Kathy," the stewardess said, "we're going to help you get home. Your mother called. She was told of the problem

78

with the plane, and she was concerned about you. We're going to have someone meet you in Louisville and help you find your plane to St. Louis. Here, this button will help them identify you."

The stewardess moved to secure the pin on Kathy's blouse. Kathy did not like the woman touching her, she did not know this woman, or the others for that matter. She did not trust them. She trusted the big lady. The big lady would take care of her, not these strangers. She began to cry.

"Kathy, it's okay," her friend said, giving a meaningful look to the stewardess. "I'll still be with you. We'll all be together. When they come to meet you, we'll just add one more to our group. It will be even better. The person who meets us will know exactly where to go. We won't have to stop and ask. It will be better for us–all of us."

Kathy looked uncertainly at the woman, then at the stewardess.

"That sounds like a good plan to me," said the stewardess.

"I won't leave you till you are with someone from your family," promised the woman.

Kathy's fears subsided, and she relaxed. She nodded. "Okay dokey."

When they finally arrived in St. Louis, eight hours late, they found Kathy's brother, Bob, asleep in a chair. It was 4:00 A.M.

"Kathy?" He cried when she woke him. "Thank God you're here. We've been worried sick about you." He looked at the woman who had obviously been helping Kathy. "How can we ever thank you?" he asked.

"I was glad to do it," she said. "Kathy's a very brave young woman traveling alone with her problem."

"Brave, yes," said Bob, "and stubborn, too. She always gets what she wants, one way or another."

The woman nodded, her earlier question answered.

"Well, I wish her the best," she said. Turning to Kathy, she gave her a hug, pressing Kathy against her ample bosom. "God bless you, Kathy. Keep on trying. Never give up," she said.

Then she turned and was gone, forever out of Kathy's life, but never out of her mind.

છ----------------------ભ

Chapter 9

THE HOMECOMING

It was one of those frigid January days. Kathy braced herself against the wind, tucking her head into the collar of her coat, and made her way into the rehabilitation building. Her feet made only slightly different prints in the snow, the dragging right foot much improved by the past four months of intensive physical therapy. Kathy struggled with the heavy door, finally pulling it open against the wind using her good left hand. Her purse, hanging precariously on her right arm, had slid down from her shoulder and banged against her as she tediously maneuvered herself into position to be able to catch the door with her body before it slammed shut again. Then she inched around it and finally got inside where it was warm.

Kathy grabbed her purse before it fell to the ground and threw it back up on her shoulder. She removed the glove from her left hand, using her teeth to inch it off. Then, with this good hand, she removed her right glove. Good, her fingers were not too red. She had to be careful of frostbite. The circulation was slow in her semi-paralyzed right hand; her fingers could easily be damaged by the cold.

That worry aside, Kathy started down the hall to her first therapy session. She was stopped by one of the nurses at the desk.

"Hi, Kathy," the nurse greeted her warmly.

"Hi." Kathy smiled. She liked this nurse. Her name was Sharon, and she always had something bright and cheery to say.

"Kathy," Sharon said, "you look nice today. Your hair is growing back into quite a cute style."

"Thanks," said Kathy, a little embarrassed at the mention of her hair. It was looking better. Thank goodness she had always had a thick bushy head of hair. It helped to fill in the dent on the left side of her head.

"Oh, Kathy, I almost forgot," added Sharon. "There's a lady from the Social Security Department here to see you. I think she wants to fill out the forms for your disability claim. You can use the nurses' office. I had her wait in there for you. And I told physical therapy you'd be a little late, okay?"

"Okay, sure," answered Kathy. She walked silently to the nurses' office just past the desk. She supposed it was okay, but she did not really like it when they just arranged things and then told her about them later. Kathy used to love surprises, but since the accident, she preferred—she needed—a neat, orderly existence. Something like this, any new experience, threw her off kilter. She could not think quickly enough to adjust immediately to new situations. She needed time to sort them out.

In this frame of mind, Kathy apprehensively entered the nurses' office. She was greeted by a middle-aged woman in a tweed suit.

"Hello, you must be Kathy," the woman smiled, and extended her hand, but Kathy did not respond.

"You are Kathy Hughes, aren't you?" the woman asked again, this time with a slight chill in her voice. She let the hand fall to her side.

"Yes," answered Kathy with uneasiness in her voice.

"Well, good, then," said the woman, assuming an efficient attitude. "We should probably just get started then. I know you have an appointment in physical therapy. Why don't we sit down?" She pointed to a chair.

Kathy sat down and started to take off her coat, a procedure that was longer and more involved than the woman would have liked. She shifted uncomfortably in her chair until Kathy had finished.

"Well, now," she said. "I think the nurse told you—we just have to have you fill out these forms. They're for your social security disability claim. Then, of course, it will take a while for them to be processed, and you will hear from us as soon as that is done."

Kathy just stared at the woman.

"Do you understand?" asked the woman, leaning forward in her chair.

"Yes," said Kathy. She was still staring at the woman.

"Is something wrong?" the woman asked.

"No." Kathy answered. She did not like the woman, but she would not say so. She wished the nurse had stayed with her. She felt alone and abandoned.

The woman cleared her throat. "Your full name is Margaret Kathryn Hughes; is that correct?"

"Yes," answered Kathy.

"Your address?"

"I living with my Mom," said Kathy.

"What is the street address, the house number?" pressed the woman.

"Umm... I... it's..." Kathy stammered. The woman waited.

"Don't know," said Kathy, finally, looking at the floor.

"You don't know or you can't remember?" asked the woman.

"Can't 'member," said Kathy, her face turning red. She was annoyed. She knew her address. They had been working on it in therapy. Why couldn't she remember?

"Well, never mind, Kathy. I can get it off your records," said the lady. "But I do need some other information that I can't get from there. Can you tell me about your accident? When did it happen?"

"Summer, nighttime, August," answered Kathy, proud of herself.

"Yes, okay, but what was the date and the time of the accident?"

Kathy became flustered. Date... time? She did not know these things. They weren't important. The accident was over. Learning was important now–therapy, speaking. That was important–not these questions that made her feel dumb. Why was this lady keeping her from therapy, anyway? She did not want any more questions.

"Done," said Kathy.

The woman started to speak.

"No, done," repeated Kathy, starting to struggle out of her seat. The woman was wasting Kathy's time, and she did not have time to waste. She had work to do.

"You know we can't process your claim without getting these questions answered, Ms. Hughes," the woman said, annoyance creeping into her voice.

Kathy stopped. She looked directly at the woman. "Don't know date... t-time," she said.

The woman softened. "Perhaps we are going about this the wrong way," she said. "I think maybe it would work better if I talked with someone from your family, instead. You said you live with your Mom?"

Kathy nodded.

"Well, I'll get in touch with her then, and we'll get the forms filled out another day."

Kathy sniffled. "Okay" she said.

"I'm sorry, Kathy," the woman began.

"S'okay" said Kathy. She struggled with the door.

"Here, let me help you," said the woman, opening the door for her.

"Thanks," said Kathy. She walked out and didn't look back.

By the time Kathy got through her first therapy session, she had put the incident with the woman out of her mind. *I don't want to think about it, she had told herself. Makes me upset. I'm not going to think about bad, sad things. I'm just going to think about getting better.*

৪০--------------------গ৪

Virginia knew Kathy needed more treatment than the rehabilitation center at St. John's could offer. She had been working steadily, ever since the accident, at locating a facility that was better equipped to handle Kathy's unique needs. She discovered that in the United States there were two resident centers for aphasic patients where therapy was strictly for aphasics and the therapy centered around the aphasics' specific needs for coping in everyday life. One of these centers was in Ann Arbor, Michigan, easily accessible. It sounded like just what Kathy needed—a place where she could be with others like her, where she could learn specific coping skills, related to her individual needs, a place to live and work at the same time, a place where she could feel "normal" once again.

Virginia called Kathy's surgeon, Dr. Andrews, and asked if he would give Kathy the recommendation she needed to get into the aphasia center. He agreed, but they needed to bring Kathy to his office for an evaluation and to fill out the forms.

So in March, 1980, Kathy and her mother went back to Port Clinton. It had been only three months since Kathy's earlier plane trip, and the memory of the confusing flight made Kathy uneasy. But this time as she boarded the plane, her mother by her side, Kathy was sure nothing would go wrong.

Sure enough, they got to Port Clinton without incident, and Kathy relaxed. They stayed with a friend who had an apartment near Kathy's old one. Kathy was anxious to see her old neighbors and friends.

The following day, Kathy and Virginia drove to Dr. Andrews' office. Dr. Andrews had already made preliminary arrangements with Ann Arbor, and Kathy was to be accepted at the aphasia center. He signed the final forms and gave them to Virginia. Now Kathy was on the waiting list. Unfortunately, the aphasia center housed only about twelve patients at a time, and it might be up to a year before Kathy could get in. Kathy would have to continue therapy elsewhere for some time yet.

Disappointed about the wait, but glad to get into this specialized program, Kathy went back to her friend's house, feeling that at least she was moving forward. She would continue with the work they gave her in St. Louis and hope for signs of progress. But her real hope lay in the aphasia center, where she felt her condition would be understood, where *she* would be understood.

In this early stage, Kathy tended to downplay her own progress, perhaps because it was so slow compared to anything else she had ever done. In reality, she had made real gains in her therapy at St. Louis. She had been almost totally out of touch with the rest of the world when she started. Now she was speaking some and learning the basics of reading and writing. She had come a long way. But in her own mind it was never enough. Kathy still often thought of herself as she was before the accident, and by comparison, the gains she was making seemed small.

After dinner, Kathy thought about paying Bill a surprise visit. His trailer was not far away. She could easily walk there. She had not talked with him since her visit in December, and he did not know she was here. Wouldn't it be fun to see the surprise and excitement on his face when he answered the door and saw her standing there? She thought it was a great idea, more fun than she had had in a long time, too long, in fact. That settled it; she was going to do it.

Virginia looked worried, but Kathy assured her she knew the way and would be perfectly safe. And Bill would walk her home. Kathy put on a new sweater that her Mom had given her for their trip. She fussed with her hair and sprayed on cologne. Finally she decided she was ready. Her heart pounding, she walked the few blocks to Bill's place, hardly noticing anything except her own intense emotions.

She knocked on the door, but no one answered. Bill's car was there, and the lights were on. She figured he must be in the shower. Bill often showered at night because he had to get up so early in the mornings for work. She knocked once more, then tried the door knob. It was unlocked. Her heart fluttering, Kathy entered the trailer.

"Bill?" she called out. "Bill, are you here?"

At first everything was quiet, but then Kathy heard shuffling sounds from the bedroom. Bill's voice called out, "Hey, who's out there?"

Kathy was silent. She did not want to miss her moment. Let him come out so she could see him first.

Cursing, Bill came through the bedroom door into the living area. His mouth dropped open and his eyes grew wide.

"Kathy, my God. What are you doing here?" he asked.

"Surprise!" Kathy shouted as she ran to him, throwing her arms around him.

Kathy leaned her head on Bill's shoulder for a moment. Then she froze. Beyond her, in the bedroom, she saw someone else. It was a woman.

"Who... who's th-that?" Kathy stammered, beginning to cry. *Oh, no, he wouldn't. He couldn't be doing this to me—not now.*

"Hey, Kathy, I'm sorry. But you didn't even call. I mean, it's been months since we even talked..." Bill's voice trailed off as they both watched the girl enter the room. She was tucking her shirt into her jeans.

"I know when I'm not *wanted*," she quipped. "See ya later, Bill. Call me again sometime."

Something inside Kathy exploded. She wanted to tear the girl's hair out—to tear her apart. She struggled to get loose, but Bill was holding her back.

"Let it go, Kathy," he said.

"Damn! Damn you! Damn! Damn! Kathy screamed at the girl's back as she retreated out the door.

Then, sobbing, Kathy faced Bill. How could he have betrayed her so?

Chapter 10

NEVER LOOK BACK

Sobbing into her mother's shoulder on the plane ride back, Kathy related the scene at Bill's apartment. Virginia's heart ached, feeling her daughter's pain.

"Maybe you're better off this way, Kathy," Virginia soothed, trying to sound logical. "If Bill can't handle the situation, it's best that you find out now."

Virginia had had her doubts about Bill's fidelity over the past months. She had even had doubts before the accident, but knowing Kathy's obsession with Bill, she dared not voice her fears. And when she had found out about Kathy's pregnancy, she pushed her fears aside and hoped that fatherhood would bring out the best in Bill.

But now there was no baby. And Bill was *not* at his best, Virginia was sure. She wished she could talk Kathy out of wanting him, but she knew it would be useless. If only Kathy could see things realistically. Bill had never been settled. He was never the type to stay at home by the fireside. And now Kathy would not be able to live the kind of life he enjoyed. She would be a responsibility, a liability—something Bill had not bargained for.

"No, Bill's diff... nt," sobbed Kathy. She wanted her mother to understand. She was trying to tell her the whole story, but her mother seemed only to hear that Bill had hurt her terribly.

"S'okay," said Kathy, blowing her nose. "I talked with Bill. Bill ch-change. Promise."

Bill had promised. After the girl had left, Bill and Kathy had talked, Bill doing most of the talking and Kathy listening. He felt terrible that Kathy had seen this and that she felt so abandoned. But it was not really what she thought. The girl meant nothing to him. She was just a passing fling. Kathy mattered to him. He cared about her. He was sorry he had hurt her. He promised to do better. He would wait for Kathy to get better, and things would be like they used to be.

Bill had said these things. He had made promises. So it was all okay. Kathy was still hurt; she had been dealt a terrible blow. But the important thing was that it was over. Bill would never hurt her again. Kathy wanted to tell her mother all this, to convince her that Bill would change. But she could not find the words, and Kathy wasn't sure she could have been convincing even if she could talk.

℘--------------------℃

Kathy returned to St. Louis and therapy. She went to the hospital during the day, and she did homework every evening. She immersed herself in therapy, her determination driving her. But sometimes she could not keep her mind on her work. She kept wandering off into daydreams–memories of Bill and happier times. She lost her focus, and the constant grind began to get on her nerves. Soon her determination gave way to frustration: Kathy had had enough.

Kathy had only been back in St. Louis two months, but she decided to call it quits. She was sick of therapy. She thought she was not making enough progress. She would be going to Ann Arbor someday. It could be a year from now; maybe longer. But Kathy did not care any more. She had had all she could take. She wanted to go home and try it on her own. She wanted to see what she could do.

Kathy had made up her mind. There was no stopping her. So on a bright day in May, Kathy's brother, Ed, drove her back to Port Clinton, where her old cottage was still available. Kathy moved back in. It was a quiet time, a simple time, and Kathy did okay, better than expected.

She had her friends in Sandpiper Court to watch over her, and Kathy's needs had always been simple. She ate fruit and cheese and sandwiches. Sometimes she heated up soup, but she rarely cooked a meal. She still had to watch her weight. That had not changed, and besides, her friends often invited her to dinner.

But for the most part, she kept to herself, enjoying the quiet beauty of the lake, sitting out on her porch every evening to watch the sun set over Lake Erie. With no job to report to every morning, Kathy had time on her hands for the first time she could remember. But ever since the accident, she appreciated the slower pace. Alone, she could take her time to do things, not feeling pressured by someone waiting on her or watching her. There were no expectations. No one was disappointed when she "had a bad day" and all the progress she had made seemed to fly out the window.

Kathy enjoyed making her own place in the world, discovering her own capacities, and she enjoyed doing it by herself. She liked to rely on herself, to be proud of herself. She liked to be in control of her life. Not that she didn't have doubts at times. There were days when everything seemed to go wrong, and she wanted to run home to her mother. But Kathy valued her privacy above all else, and this was her home, where she belonged; she would stay.

Sometimes Kathy would wake up, and her mind would be jumbled. It would take her a few minutes to arrange her thoughts. She had been taught to think in terms of sequence. *What do I do first when I wake up?* Kathy would ask herself. An urgency in her bladder would reminder her–*oh, yes, first I go to the bathroom.* That task accomplished, her sense of habit would usually take over, and Kathy would brush her teeth, wash her face, and start to get dressed.

It was not too hard to clean up with only one good hand, but Kathy's real problems came when it was time to get dressed. Unbuttoning her pajama top with one hand, she would pull and tug and shake her shoulders until it finally dropped off. Then she would push down her bottoms and squirm out of them. Normally, Kathy wore shirts with buttons, and she would spend a half-hour or more working the buttons into the buttonholes. But she had time, and it was a challenge for Kathy to do as many things as possible in the same way she did them before the accident. Once dressed, Kathy thought about her day. What would she do next? If she felt hungry, she ate–maybe a banana or a pear and some milk. She got into the habit of turning on the TV to listen to the morning talk shows. Often they spoke too fast for her, and she did not understand everything they said. But she got the gist of it, and she thought it kept her in touch with the outside world.

Kathy knew better than to let her mind stand idle. So although she had called a hiatus on speech and occupational therapy, she did go to physical therapy at the local hospital and she did work on her own. Jean had given Kathy a "Speak & Spell" when she left St. Louis. Kathy was thrilled with it. It was actually a child's toy, meant to help very young kids learn to spell. A computerized voice would ask how to spell a simple word–"how do you spell 'apple'?" Kathy could then push the buttons on the keyboard. If she was correct, the toy would answer, "Correct, very good." If her answer was wrong, the machine said, "Sorry, that is not correct. Try again." Kathy loved it because she could work alone and at her own pace. She spent hours each day working with her Speak & Spell.

Another important tool in Kathy's work was her tape recorder. Jean had given it to her, along with a few tapes. Kathy's world opened up when she discovered tape recording. Kathy used the tapes to keep in contact with her family. She could talk when she was at her best, making fewer mistakes. And with the rewind button, she could go back and start over as often as she needed in order to get her message the way she wanted it. It was a long and arduous task to make a tape, but Kathy was always proud of the final product–an entire message, spoken coherently, understandable to anyone. Taping became a way of life with Kathy. She taped messages to herself, to remind herself of tasks. She taped music and TV programs so that she could listen to them over and over. She asked her friends to send her tape recorded letters. Taping was a lifeline for Kathy, her connection with the outside world.

As her slow motion life continued, Kathy learned to cope with her daily routine. She became more confident and started to feel like getting back into life again. Her only contacts with the outside world were her therapy and outings to her friends' houses for dinner or cards. Kathy used to love to play cards, and although she often made mistakes, she was learning to play simple card games again like "Old Maid" and "War". As Kathy grew more confident in her ability to care for herself she began to long for companionship, for someone to share her feelings with.

Bill had come to visit infrequently, only a few times a month since Kathy had been home. This bothered her, but she knew he felt uneasy around her since he was not used to seeing her this way, and she was embarrassed also. So she did not press him. His reluctance to visit made Kathy realize that she had to get better than she was. She could take a breather, but she could not stop. Perhaps it was time to *really* get back to work. Kathy thought of re-entering therapy. Perhaps it would be easier this time; she felt more sure of herself, more her own person.

Virginia had been thinking the same thing. The year or more of waiting for the Ann Arbor center was too long for Kathy to stand still. She had to keep pushing ahead, to keep moving forward, however slow the progress. Virginia consulted with Kathy's doctor from St. John's Hospital and asked him to do whatever he could to get Kathy into therapy somewhere else while she was waiting for a spot in the aphasia center in Ann Arbor.

As the summer drew to a close, Kathy had spent three months alone since the accident. She was unsure about her future plans, but she was certain of one thing; she could do it; she could live alone.

೫⦿--------------------⦿೫

Late in the summer of 1980, Kathy's family took their usual vacation, spending three weeks at their summer cottage on Lake Erie's Catawba Island. Kathy went to the cottage to spend the vacation time with her family.

It did not turn out to be much of a vacation for Kathy, however. She had some unfinished business to take care of. She had been walking around with a large section of her brain unprotected, where her fractured skull bone had been removed. It had been a year since her accident, and now this problem had to be addressed.

Dr. Andrews was to perform a second surgery on Kathy's skull to insert a special, molded plastic plate over her exposed brain. A dentist would make an impression of the dent in her head, and the plate would be manufactured from this mold. Virginia and Kathy would spend much of their vacation preparing for the surgery. Kathy did not like the idea, but she knew it had to be done.

The night before they were to go to the dentist's office to take the impression, Virginia shaved Kathy's head. It was terrible. Virginia's stomach was in knots as she took the scissors and barber's shears into Kathy's room. She wanted to be brave so that she would not upset Kathy, but her hands were trembling.

"Are you ready, Kathy?" she asked. Kathy was solemn, sitting rigidly upright on the edge of the bed.

"Yes," she said.

Virginia swallowed hard, tears filling her eyes. She dreaded this task. It had almost been possible to forget about the dent in Kathy's head because her hair had grown back so thick. Her exposed scalp would be a brutal reminder, a harsh encounter with reality. It brought back memories, memories of the accident, of Kathy's broken, bloodied body. But she had been through crises before. *You just do what you have to do,* she thought, and she started cutting.

The sound of the barber's shears shaving away the last of Kathy's hair could be heard buzzing through the thin walls of the cottage. In the next bedroom, Kathy's youngest sister, Laura, heard the noise and wondered what was going on. She went to check it out.

"Kathy? Mom?" Laura called out as she tentatively stuck her head around the corner to look into Kathy's room. "What's going on?" Laura's mouth dropped as a look of horror crossed her face.

She screamed.

Dropping the shears, Virginia ran to Laura and pulled the child's head to her chest. "It's okay, Laura. Don't worry. Kathy's okay," she said soothingly. "We're just shaving her head so Dr. Andrews can help Kathy. He will make her safe. She won't have to wear the football helmet after that, ever again.

"Really?" asked Laura. She had always felt funny seeing Kathy in a football helmet when they rode in the car together.

"Yes, really," said Virginia, smiling.

"I'm okay," said Kathy. "See?" She had taken a scarf that Virginia had brought her and put it over her head. It was lopsided, but it covered the pink, dented flesh of Kathy's head.

Laura laughed. "You look funny," she said.

Kathy laughed too.

Thank God, she can still laugh, thought Virginia. And thank God the cutting was over. She had been sickened by the sight–the ugly pink scar zigzagging across what seemed a cavernous dent in her daughter's skull. The whole lower left side of Kathy's head was misshaped. Virginia shuddered at the thought.

"Well, let's not stay up here all night," she said, trying to sound cheerful. "I'm going downstairs for cookies and milk. Who wants to join me?"

Laura jumped up and down. "Me, me," she squealed.

Kathy and Virginia exchanged a look over Laura's head. Oh, the innocence of youth, it seemed to say. They each longed for that luxury for themselves.

Kathy became restless. They had had their cookies and

milk, and Laura had gone to bed, satisfied that everything was going to be okay with Kathy. Two of Kathy's brothers shared her restless feelings as the three of them tried to maintain their interest in a game of cards.

"I've had enough of this," Kathy's brother, Ed, finally said. "Hey, Mike, want to go out for a drink?" Then he looked at Kathy. "Kathy, what do you say? Are you up to it? Want to join us?"

"Sure," said Kathy, relieved not to be left behind.

"Well, great," answered Mike. "Let's go."

They drove to Geno's, a small local bar that served pizza and beer. They sat for a while drinking beer and listening to the juke box.

After the dinner crowd had cleared out, the bar suddenly got quiet, and Mike said, "Hey, let's move on. How about going to Ricki's for a while?"

"Sure," said Ed, and they left.

At Ricki's the crowd was just starting to build. Voices could be heard shouting over the loud music as early arrivals called out to their friends that were now arriving.

Mike found a table for them near the back, away from the jukebox and ordered them each a beer. "This place is jumping tonight," said Ed, as his eyes searched the crowd for familiar faces. "Hey, Jeff, how ya doin'?" he called out.

"Ed, old boy, what's new?" came the reply as the tall blond figure made his way to their table.

"Not much," said Ed. "You remember my brother, Mike, and my sister, Kathy, don't you?"

"Sure," said Jeff "Nice to see you again." Then to Kathy, "Uh, hey, Kathy, I was sorry to hear about your accident. But you're lookin' real good now." His eyes were focused directly on Kathy's head where the scarf covered the tell-tale scar.

She looked back at Jeff and he lowered his eyes, embarrassed to have been caught staring.

"Do you see much of Bill these days, Kathy?" he asked. Kathy and Bill's relationship was as widely known in the small town of Catawba as it was in Port Clinton. They were both tiny resort towns, not far apart, and it did not take long for news to travel from one place to the other.

"See Bill little," answered Kathy, embarrassed by his direct question.

"I see," said Jeff, and he gave Mike a meaningful look, quickly tilting his head in the direction of the bar.

Mike picked up on Jeff's cue. He looked towards the bar. There, at the far end of the bar was Bill, leaning over a short brunette with a wild hairdo. He appeared to be completely absorbed in what she was saying. As she talked, he was running his finger up and down the inside of her arm.

Mike stiffened. He looked over at Kathy. She had not seen it. Jeff was leaving and Mike gave Ed the same flick of the head that Jeff had given him.

"Hey, Ed, I'm kind of tired. What do you say we call it a night?"

"Sure," said Ed, now wise to the reason for Mike's request.

"Just get there," said Kathy, bewildered by their sudden change of heart.

"No matter, Kathy. Let's go, please?" Ed said in his most appealing voice.

Kathy stood up to leave, but just as she turned to pick up her purse, she saw Bill.

"Well," she said, her voice like ice. "See now." Slowly she started toward the bar.

"Kathy, wait!" cried Ed, but she did not hear him. Her ears were ringing with the sound of her own heartbeat.

Kathy reached the bar and stood directly in front of Bill and the girl. He did not move his hand off the girl's arm.

"Want t-talk," Kathy stammered, struggling to maintain control of herself. "Side," she added, and tilted her head toward the door.

"Sure, Kathy," Bill drawled. He had obviously been drinking for quite a while.

Barely controlling her rage, Kathy turned away and

walked toward the door.

"I'll be right back," Bill promised as he left the girl.

Mike and Ed caught up with Kathy and followed her out, trying to talk her into leaving. Kathy shook her head and kept walking. Tears welled in her eyes, but she refused to cry. When she reached the outside door, she shoved against it with her good arm, flinging it open. She walked out a way on the gravel drive and whirled around to face Bill, who was trailing behind her, swaying slightly.

"Have good time, Bill?" she demanded. "Good... good time Bill?" she spat, trying to get a reaction from him.

Bill just shrugged.

Kathy, beside herself with humiliation and rage, tried to swing at Bill, but her brothers held her back. *Oh why can't I talk?* she thought in despair. She wanted to tell him all she felt right now–the anger, the pain, the resentment.

So this is the way it is, she thought to herself. *While I'm suffering, trying to get better for him, he's out having a good time.* He doesn't care, she thought, and the realization was like a knife in her heart. *I'm suffering a living hell every day of my life, and he's out partying. He doesn't care about my pain. He doesn't care about me. God, why was I so blind?*

She struggled to get her feelings across to Bill, using her meager supply of words.

"Bill fun while Kathy hurts," she cried, her voice breaking. "You want see hurt, Bill? Want see my head?"

"No," Bill said quietly, some of his earlier confidence now gone.

"Well, going see it. Going see it!" she screamed at him as she let go of all her frustration and rage, flinging the scarf off her head, exposing the ugly reality to Bill.

Bill stared at Kathy's dented, lopsided head for a moment. Then he turned and walked away.

Trembling, Kathy took a deep breath and looked at her brothers.

"What do you want to do, Kathy?" Mike asked gently.

"Drink. Drink," said Kathy.

They went back into the bar. Sipping her drink, Kathy's thoughts seemed clearer then they had been for a long time. Fool, she thought to herself. *I've been a fool. I've lied to myself. I've been hiding my head in the sand. Bill is not the man I've always wanted him to be. Maybe he never was. I have been blinded by my obsession with him. I overlooked his weaknesses. I never saw his flaws. I was willing to forgive and forget.*

Well, no more! Ever since the accident, Bill has brought me nothing but trouble and pain. Well, I don't need more trouble and pain. I've got enough, all my own. What I do need is to get on with my life. My life, doing what I need to do to get better for me. For so long I've lived my life for Bill. What about me? Isn't it time I thought about me, Kathy, and what I'm supposed to do with my life?

God, you're really testing me aren't you? She silently asked. *I see I'm not to be a mother. I'm not even to be a wife, it seems, at least for now. Well, what, what in heaven's name do you want me to do?*

Kathy pondered this question, searching for an answer in her mind, but finding none. Then out of the darkness of her inner self, she felt welcoming warmth spread through her, illuminating her mind. A tiny voice seemed to whisper, "Just get better and the rest will follow."

I will get better, Kathy vowed to herself. I will get better for me.

The girl that Bill had been talking to walked up to Kathy. "Do you know where Bill is?" she asked.

"Don't know," said Kathy. "Don't care."

And she meant it.

Chapter 11

LEARNING INDEPENDENCE AT RUSK REHAB

The sound of familiar voices woke Kathy from a drugged sleep. She struggled to bring her mind into focus.

"Mmm . . . Rich," she mumbled, recognizing her brother's voice first. Then she smiled. "Hi, Doc."

Dr. Andrews is here. It must be morning already. He always comes in so early. Busy, busy. Hearing her name, Kathy turned her attention to what Dr. Andrews was saying.

"Kathy's coming along quite well here. I'm pleased with the healing of her incision. The plate is stable, and she's healing rapidly. In fact, I see no reason why she can't go home to your cottage to be with the family for the weekend. We can remove the stitches sometime next week on an outpatient basis."

"Great! Thanks, Doctor," said Rich. Then he turned to Kathy. "Kathy, you get to go home for the weekend. Isn't that great?"

"S 'okay," Kathy said with little enthusiasm.

Rich looked puzzled. "You do want to go home, don't you, Kathy? You were so anxious to get out of the hospital last time, I thought you'd be excited. Are you feeling okay? Maybe you're not up to the crowd at home. Is that it?"

"Well, she could stay here if she doesn't feel she can handle it," said Dr. Andrews. "We're in no hurry to push her out."

"It's up to you, Kathy," Rich told her. "Think about it for a while. You don't have to decide now. We'll talk about it later."

Dr. Andrews and Rich left. Kathy thought about going home, and she was puzzled herself by her mixed feelings. *You'd better believe I wanted out last time,* she thought, remembering her two attempts at escape. *But that was*

99

because I wanted to get to Bill. How crazy I was. I could have killed myself and for what? Look at me now—left alone, dumped. Well, I'm not going to think about that now.

Kathy wiped a tear from her eye and sighed. *It's all so different this time,* she thought. *I'm not wild to get out because I have no reason to be. And it is so peaceful here, so quiet, so comfortable. The nurses take good care of me. I have no worries. I could just stay here for a while longer and relax. That would be nice.*

Then Kathy thought of her family at Catawba. Their vacation was almost over. They would be going back to Missouri soon. She knew her mother was anxious to see her home, to know that she was okay. She wanted to see her family too, but they were so noisy, not like here, where it was quiet. At the hospital Kathy could think.

Kathy had done a lot of thinking the past few days, since her confrontation with Bill. Mostly she had thought about herself, her life, her future. Bill was history. She was done with him. She had to move on. She had done it alone before, a long time ago. Of course, that was before the accident. But she knew that if she could do it then, she could do it now. Kathy took a deep breath and felt a sense of pride well up inside her. *I have a challenge,* she thought, *a personal challenge, for the first time since the accident.*

Kathy did go home for the weekend. It seemed to be the simplest thing to do. She did not want her family to worry about her, and she did not feel like trying to explain her sudden change of heart concerning hospitals.

The following week, after most of her family had left, Kathy returned to the hospital to get the stitches removed from her incision. Then for the second time, she started the long process of growing a new head of hair,

Virginia's persistent search for a new therapy program had paid off. With the help of Kathy's doctor from St. John's, Kathy was enrolled in a program at University of Missouri–Columbia. It was a five-week, intensive inpatient program, with additional therapy on an outpatient basis as needed following the discharge from the hospital. Rusk Rehabilitation Center at University of Missouri–Columbia, one hundred miles from St. Louis, was to be Kathy's home for the next several months.

Saying goodbye was becoming easier for Kathy, as once again she went back to Port Clinton, packed up her belongings, and left her home. *I'll be back,* she swore to herself. *Someday I'll be back for good.*

At least her new residence had the familiar sights and sounds of a hospital. Kathy had begun to appreciate the security and stability of a hospital setting. In the hospital, Kathy could focus all of her attention on her work. Things were orderly, precise, and quiet, like a sanctuary removed from the demands of the real world. Without the distractions, she thought she could make bigger strides in her recovery. The challenge had begun.

Kathy's first roommate was an eighteen-year-old girl who had injured her head in a car accident. But unlike Kathy, this girl had not been lucky. Her fiancée was killed in the accident and she lay in a semi comatose state. Any communication she might have been able to manage was silenced by a tracheotomy tube in her throat. Kathy pitied the girl.

She has no life at all, thought Kathy. *The nurses do everything for her. At least I can take care of myself. I get around. I do things. At least I have a chance at life. Thank God I can help myself.*

And she did. Kathy spared herself no pain, no embarrassment. *Whatever it takes,* she often said to herself as her physical therapist put her through grueling routines. She crawled around on the floor like a baby, oblivious to how silly she may have looked, knowing only that somehow this was supposed to help. She walked and walked, up and down the physical therapy ramp and in the hospital corridors, trying to improve her stride.

About two weeks into the program at Rusk, Kathy started to become frustrated with her progress in

Occupational Therapy. In O.T., although Kathy was given simple crafts to work on that did require her to use her disabled hand, she was given none of the muscle exercises she had become used to in other therapy sessions. This annoyed her. She believed that working at crafts was a waste of time and that she was not being given individual attention from the O.T. therapist. Kathy had lately become very goal oriented. If she could not see the end result of a task, she did not think it had merit. She could see no benefit from sitting around doing what she called "busywork." She had no time for busy work. It was unfair that she should be forced to waste her time–time that she could be spending on other types of therapy.

Kathy brought these complaints to Pat, her language disorders therapist. She felt that Pat was her friend. She could open up to her.

"Hate O.T., no go," Kathy cried during one of their two-hour sessions.

"Now, Kathy," said Pat, "you can't mean that. You know *all* your therapies are important. And even though you don't see the reason behind it, your craft projects are an important part of helping you recover. Think for a moment. Don't you use your right hand when you do those projects?"

Kathy nodded her head yes.

"See, you are working with your muscles." Pat laughed. "Kathy, all therapy doesn't have to be painful and difficult. It can be fun. Besides, don't you feel proud when you've finished something and you've done a good job?"

Kathy looked at Pat. She was beginning to get the picture. "Okay," she said smiling. "Okay. Okay. Work."

"You'd work twenty-four hours a day if we'd let you, wouldn't you Kathy?" Pat asked, only half-joking.

"Yes," answered Kathy, and she was not joking at all.

Kathy had been asking for extra homework the past few days. Even with most of her days strictly programmed, Kathy still found herself getting done early with the work that she was given to do on her own. She wanted more, enough to keep her busy right up to bedtime. She would not waste a moment of the precious time she had for relearning the skills that would make her independent again.

"Okay, let's get started then," said Pat. They were in a tiny cubicle, no more than four feet square, sitting across from each other. On the table between them lay several workbooks. Pat opened one and began the morning therapy session.

"Okay, Kathy, let's start with this word." Pat pointed in the book to the word "clock." It was written in large letters below a picture of a clock. "What is that word, Kathy? Do you remember?"

"Flies," answered Kathy. Then she shook her head. "No..." She hesitated, trying to remember. Why had she thought of a fly?

"Good, Kathy," said Pat. "You're keying in to an old saying. But what is it that flies?"

Flies, thought Kathy. Flies, *not a fly. Flies.., what flies?* Then something in Kathy's mind clicked into place time flies.

"Time," she said exuberantly.

"Great, Kathy. You've connected," said Pat, praising Kathy's conscious efforts at associating. "Now, we know it has something to do with time. What is the word? It has something to do with time. Look at the picture again. Look at the word. It starts with the letter..."

"C," said Kathy. She recognized 'C' easily. "C," she repeated. "Clock!"

"Good, Kathy. Very, very good. Now copy the word clock on your worksheet under the picture. Right there, see?"

Pat waited patiently while Kathy copied the word. Copying was not hard for Kathy. All the letters were there. You didn't have to figure out which way a 'b' or 'd' went. Writing 'd's' and 'b's' was the worst. She always got them mixed up. But copying was not at all like writing. She could not do that yet. She could not really read either.

Sometimes they said she could, but Kathy did not really think so. Sometimes she just got lucky with a word.

When she had finished, they started all over again. Sometimes they would only get through two or three words in a two-hour session. It was the repetition that helped. If she repeated a word often enough, using all of its "cues"–the picture, the letters, the beginning sound–, Kathy could eventually make the word her own, another hard earned addition to her vocabulary, another notch in the gun handle.

Sometimes they would spend the whole session working on Kathy's word memory. Kathy would listen through earphones to words being spoken. Then she would try to repeat what she had heard. As the weeks went by and Kathy progressed, they moved on to short sentences. Kathy would listen and then repeat the sentence from memory. After maybe fifty times or so, Pat would remove one word from the sentence. Kathy had to put it in, using the memory accessing skills that she was learning.

For Kathy, Pat had determined that she needed to use a combination of several modalities–motor, sight, and comprehension–all at once to help Kathy "cue into" a word. If Kathy could pick up on one cue, the other associations would come more easily.

The fact that Kathy's motor skills for writing had to be "reprogrammed" into her left hand provided an extra obstacle. Not only did Kathy's hand sometimes not want to function, as it should, at times neither did her mouth. Part of the problem was that Kathy's injury had not only affected her language center (word accessing, word choice, word memory), it had also affected her motor center for speech. Her mouth had "forgotten" how to form certain sounds. It seemed that Kathy had to fight a major battle on all fronts at once.

During the five-week, inpatient therapy, Kathy concentrated her efforts on speech, just as she had at St. John's. She slowly progressed from scrambling the letters of words ('dog' would come out as 'ogd') to speaking and copying sentences. Her syntax was far from being under control, but that might get better as time went by. Patience was Kathy's greatest attribute, patience and persistence. She knew it would all come together some day.

Kathy's social life at Rusk, such as it was, revolved around the meals she ate with the other residents and their designated "outings." On Tuesdays they would get on a bus, wheelchairs, walkers, and all, and drive over to the bowling center at the University to bowl. It was fun. It gave them a chance to relax from the rigors of therapy, and they learned to laugh at their own limitations. Wednesdays and Thursdays they played other sports, perhaps basketball or volleyball.

Kathy, who had always loved people, began to open up a bit within the protective environment of the rehabilitation center, where she felt that everyone was "just like her." She made friends with an elderly man who was outgoing and friendly, but who always seemed to be alone. One night he asked her if she wanted to go to a campus movie theater. Kathy was reluctant to go outside the rehabilitation building without the comfort of the group escort, but the man looked so eager.

"Fine, okay," she finally said. They saw the movie "Meatballs," a comedy. Kathy laughed and laughed, partly at the movie, partly for the sheer joy of laughing again.

Another friendship began at dinner one evening. Kathy was sitting alone when a new girl walked by. She looked at Kathy, smiling slightly, then looked at the floor. She began to move away, but Kathy called out to her.

"Sit up?" she asked. Then catching her mistake, Kathy laughed, not bothering to try to correct it. She was certain the girl would understand. Mismatched prepositions were common around there.

The girl laughed too, and sat down.

"Name?" questioned Kathy.

"Ann," answered the girl.

In bits and pieces of conversation, Kathy and Ann

pieced together their past histories and discovered they had a common bond. They both used to love playing chess. In fact, Ann had been a state champion in her league. They decided to try playing a game. Kathy had not played chess since before the accident. She did not know if she would remember how. Ann had a brain tumor, but her memory was intact. She would be a challenging partner.

They set up the board in the recreation room. Kathy sat for a long time looking at the pieces. Then she smiled. She made her first move. Playing chess with Ann was to become a nightly event, one that Kathy looked forward to. Ann was quite a bit younger than she, but she and Kathy became close. They exchanged bits of conversation and laughed at themselves when they made a bad move. Kathy was proud of herself when she won several games over Ann, "the champ." Because Kathy had played chess since childhood, it had become a "skill" memory–like riding a bike, once learned never forgotten.

The five weeks of inpatient therapy flew by for Kathy. Although it was arduous work, Kathy never gave up, even when she became tired and irritable and cried in frustrated anger.

"Kathy, why don't you take a break?" Pat would suggest.

"No!" Kathy would say defiantly. "Work. Talk." Her goal was always in front of her, a guiding light beckoning her, showing her the way out of the darkness.

Kathy hated to leave the protected seclusion of the hospital environment. But when her five weeks were up and the doctor insisted that Kathy was well enough to live outside the hospital and continue therapy on an outpatient basis, Kathy had no choice but to leave.

Since Kathy's family lived 125 miles away in St. Louis, Kathy had to live on her own again to continue outpatient therapy at Rusk Rehab. A long-time friend of Kathy's, who lived near Columbia, came down to help her find a suitable apartment. They circled several choices from the newspaper and went to check them out, concentrating on the apartments closest to the campus.

The first apartment was nice, but the woman who owned it seemed leery of Kathy because of her problems. She was afraid Kathy might not be able to take care of the apartment or would start a fire or something. They moved on. The next several apartments were too dirty and unkept.

Finally, back on campus again, Kathy spotted a hand printed sign. "For Rent," she said.

"Kathy, you read!" her friend Amy said, amazed and delighted. "You read the sign!"

"No, sign. Member," said Kathy, trying to downplay the incident. She had not really read the sign, she told herself. Anyone knows what a "For Rent" sign looks like. She could not read yet. Reading was too hard. No, she was not ready for that yet.

This place was perfect. Kathy could have her own room, sharing the large, old house with four other girls, all university students. She got her things and moved in.

It was a great experience for Kathy. The girls were all much younger than she, and were very sports-oriented, jogging and swimming daily. But they encouraged Kathy. They helped her with her homework and made her feel as though she belonged. Following their lead, Kathy began to go to a nearby health spa to swim and work out. She was beginning to feel more like her old self, for exercise had always been a part of Kathy's life.

She started to practice yoga again and began meditating. She wanted to find a place of peace within herself where maybe she could recapture, just for a moment, that sense of love and acceptance that she had felt in the hospital when she had realized a oneness between God and herself.

℘--------------------℃

Kathy adjusted herself to this routine and slowly gained

confidence in her ability to deal with the rest of the world. She spoke to strangers only when she had to, and she explained her obvious difficulty by simply saying, "Accident, don't talk good." Others would have to learn to accept her imperfect speech. It was the way she was, and that was that.

Kathy spent the next four months working extensively on her speech with two therapists–Mary, a speech therapist, and Pat, her language disorders therapist. Mary helped Kathy with the motor skills area of speaking, like forming sounds. She helped Kathy learn to use the muscles of her mouth and throat to make the sounds for speech. Kathy would practice making the sounds of vowels, consonants, and words. Kathy spent hours repeating the same sounds and words over and over, until finally the memory of how to produce them was reprogrammed into her brain. As the fourth month of outpatient therapy drew to a close, both Pat and Mary concluded that Kathy was reaching a plateau. She had been tested at regular intervals during therapy, and her overall test scores had improved dramatically from that first PICA test right after the accident. Kathy had rebounded from a "hopeless" six percent score on the PICA test of language ability to an overall average of about eighty percent on combined test scores measuring verbal, gestural, understanding, and graphic (writing/copying) abilities. On the whole, Kathy could now communicate and understand most messages. She could express herself effectively in small, short phrases. But on the sentence and paragraph level Kathy still became lost and confused. She used incorrect syntax. She might say, "The dog man bit," instead of "The dog bit the man." And she still could not find all the right words to get the full meaning of her message across.

Yet Kathy had surpassed the doctors' expectations. She had injured her brain and she would never be perfect. This seemed to be the point where she might level off. Given the circumstances, she seemed to have come as far as one could expect. Both Pat and Mary thought it was time for Kathy to move out of therapy and into the real world, to continue her work on her own, practicing what she had been taught in therapy. They believed that this practice might help her improve somewhat, but that further therapy would simply be a waste of time and money.

Pat tried to make Kathy understand. "Kathy," she said, "you have come so far. Look at what you've gained. When you came here, you could barely communicate; your speech was so jumbled that only the people who knew you well could understand you. You had to fight for each word you spoke. You couldn't have functioned in normal society.

"But look at you now. Sure your speech is not back to where it was, but you knew that it never would be. Be proud of what you can do, Kathy. You can talk coherently now, even if it is in small bits and pieces. You can function in the real world. Some people never even get this far, Kathy. You know that. And you've made it this far because you wanted to so badly. You worked so hard. You should be proud of what you did. But I think you've reached the point where you've completed the relearning process. Now all you need is practice."

But Kathy was adamant. She refused to believe that this was the end of the line. She argued with Pat, begging her to see it her way.

"Go Ann Arbor. Go!" Kathy had vehemently proclaimed. "Wait, wait. Now go!" Her eyes were filled with tears as she tried to make Pat understand.

A spot at Ann Arbor had opened up. Kathy wanted to take this one last chance. She wanted to travel the final leg of her journey. She believed she could leave no stone unturned, no opportunity untried. She had waited and hoped to be accepted into the program. Now that she was, she could not believe that it would be a waste of time.

"I still think you have reached your peak, Kathy," Pat said. "Any gains you make here on will be very specific to your environment, to how you live. You will adjust to your daily routine and will probably improve on the communications you use every day. But I can't foresee a big change. I'm sorry."

"Have try," said Kathy. That was all she could say about it. She had to try.

"Okay, Kathy," Pat finally conceded. "You've fooled us before. Why not try to do it again?" She smiled at Kathy, and Kathy smiled back, relieved.

"I will need some time to try to get the reports together, Kathy," Pat told her. "That means I won't be able to spend that time in therapy with you. It will take about a week. I know how you hate to miss therapy sessions, but it's either that or not get the reports done."

"S'okay," said Kathy. She knew she needed Pat's progress reports to enter the program. Although she hated to sacrifice their therapy time, Kathy saw no alternative. She knew how busy Pat was, and she could study on her own. It would be worth it; she would reenter a totally therapy oriented environment, one dedicated specifically to aphasics like herself. It would help her, she was sure. It had to. Kathy would accept no other possibility.

Chapter 12

GOALS IN ANN ARBOR WITH APHASIA

Gulping down the last bit of coffee in her cup, Kathy stood up and started across the cafeteria to the tray return area. She had passed up the many breakfast selections in the food line, taking only coffee. Breakfast was not a big meal for Kathy. In addition, she considered herself a "foodaholic." Once she started eating, she did not like to stop. So she put it off as long as possible. Besides, it was too early to eat. How could anyone be hungry at this hour, anyone, of course, except Sarah? Kathy looked at Sarah's tray as she walked past her–eggs, toast, juice, and milk. Sarah could always eat, even at the crack of dawn. *How come she never has to worry about her weight?* Kathy wondered enviously.

"Sarah, hurry. Ther... py," Kathy warned her friend. Sarah was always walking in late. Kathy did not like to be late, so she waved to her friend and kept on going.

A few steps down the hall, Kathy entered the large room where she would have her first therapy session of the day. Dan was already there. He patted the couch, indicating he wanted Kathy to sit down beside him.

"Sarah, late," Kathy said as she sat down. Dan smiled. It was a small joke between them, Sarah's consistent tardiness. It gave them something to talk about, and they enjoyed kidding Sarah. Sarah good-naturedly laughed with them.

Brenda, their group therapist, came in. "Good morning group," she said. "How's everyone this morning?"

"Good" a voice called from the doorway. Sarah slipped into a chair, giving a sly wink to Kathy as she sat down.

"Well, I'm glad we're *all* here," chided Brenda, giving Sarah a mock frown. "Now, let's see what's first on our

111

agenda today."

The "agenda" was large and varied. Here at the University of Michigan's Residential Aphasia Clinic in Ann Arbor, Kathy was doing things she had never done before. Her three-member group therapy sessions often included things like role playing and pantomimes. The three patients helped one another act out situations they might face once they got out on their own. Sometimes they gave "reports" on a TV or news program they had seen the night before.

Kathy had given her first report four months earlier. She had watched a TV sitcom intently, trying to remember every detail. The therapist had picked this particular program because it had special significance for all of them. The show concerned several high school girls who lived together in a private boarding school. A friend of one of the girls came for a visit. She was a handicapped person. Watching the reactions of the other girls as they moved from embarrassment to understanding to acceptance, Kathy felt a bond with the handicapped girl. She realized how hard it was for the others to accept someone who was not "normal." She saw that she would have to meet people more than half way if she was to avoid embarrassment. As with the handicapped girl, Kathy knew that the more people understood her condition and the more open Kathy herself was about her limitations, the easier it would be to function in society.

These were the insights Kathy wanted to share with the group. But the next day in therapy, when it came her turn to report, Kathy floundered. She knew what she wanted to say, the words, the feelings she wanted to express. But she could not get it out.

"Sympathize," Kathy said. "Urn... urn..." She raised her right hand and, circling it around, placed it palm out in front of her. "Wait a minute. Hold on. I'll get it," the gesture said.

The group patiently waited as Kathy searched her memory for the words to express herself. Remnants of her thoughts the night before raced through her mind. She had the essence of it, if only she could get the details.

"No feelings," she said finally. Yes, that was part of it, but she wanted to say more.

"Right, Kathy. Good," Brenda, Kathy's therapist at the time, said. "You can understand the girl's feelings and empathize with her."

"Sympathize and empathize," Kathy said.

"Right. Now, what else? What other ideas did the movie bring out?"

Kathy thought, something about the show had frustrated her, what was it?

"Friends try hardly," she added.

"Do you mean the girl's friends hardly tried. They didn't try hard enough, they needed to try harder?" asked Brenda.

"Yes."

"Okay. Harder at what, Kathy?" she prompted.

"Harder understand."

"Harder at understanding. Okay. Understanding what, Kathy?"

On and on they went, Kathy expressing her impressions in two to three word phrases and Brenda digging out more details. Kathy had felt terribly inadequate. She had more to say, more to contribute. The feeling of being trapped inside an inadequate body suddenly overwhelmed Kathy. *Will it always be like this?* she wondered. *Will I never be able to share my feelings again? I cannot bear to live like that,* she thought.

Today, four months later, things were much different. Kathy was moving ahead in all areas. She was no longer limited to two or three word phrases. She was working on talking in sentences. She was listening and understanding whole paragraphs. Brenda had been replaced by Joy. Joy, contrary to what her name implied, was not as bubbly or vivacious as Brenda had been. Joy was much more work oriented and concentrated on what they called the graphic skills–reading and writing. Each new five-week semester brought new therapists with new ideas. The group was adjusting to Joy's way of doing things.

They were working on sentence structure. Joy had given them each a worksheet with several sentences written on it. The words of the sentence were out of order. The group had to identify the basic elements of the sentence—the noun, verb, adjective, etc.—and then rewrite the sentence in the proper order.

"Yuk. Like school, fourth grade," complained Sarah.

"Fifth grade maybe," answered Kathy. "I liked school." Kathy had always been good at diagramming sentences in grade school. She felt confident and in control during these sessions.

Sarah gave Kathy a doubtful look and went back to her own work.

Kathy finished her first sentence. "A stone rolling moss no gathers" became "A rolling stone gathers no moss." She immediately went to work on the next two, marking 'n' for noun, 'v' for verb, 'a' for adverb, and 'aj' for adjective above the appropriate words. Then she unscrambled the sentences. "A penny saved a penny is earned" became "A penny saved is a penny earned." "Smell flowers the time to take" became "Take time to smell the flowers." Kathy raised her hand.

"Done, Kathy?" Joy asked, nodding her head in approval. "Here, try this one." Joy had an extra worksheet set aside. She figured that Kathy might finish well ahead of the others, and she knew about Kathy's intolerance for wasting time.

Sarah gave Kathy a rueful smile. *Finished first again, huh?* it seemed to say. Kathy smiled back, an encouraging smile. She was elated with her own progress. She was making real improvements in all areas—speech, reading, comprehension, and even a little in writing. She was thrilled to see the gap between herself and other "normal" people closing somewhat. But it bothered Kathy that she was leaving Sarah behind. Sarah had been slowly improving, especially in speech, but not nearly as quickly as Kathy. She saw that the difference was starting to create a gap between the two of them. Sarah was Kathy's only real friend here in Ann Arbor, and she hated to see that happen. But nothing must stop her from moving ahead. With a sigh, Kathy bent over her work.

When they had all finished, Joy went over their work with them, making sure that each of them understood and corrected any mistakes.

Then she asked, "Can anyone tell me the meaning of the first sentence?"

Kathy raised her hand again.

"Okay, Kathy," Joy said.

"Means you stay on movin, you don't get... barnacles... no... attached?" Kathy exclaimed. Well that was almost what she meant. She wanted to say that if you are a roamer, like she once was, you never get any attachments–to places or people. But it was close enough, better than before at any rate.

"Good, Kathy," Joy said. "Now who can explain the meaning of the next sentence?"

As the semester went on, Joy worked with Kathy's group to identify errors in word use, perhaps an incorrect verb or pronoun. Sentences like "She wanted to catch his own fish" gave all of them problems. Kathy still had trouble with pronouns.

The therapists tried to orient the work as much as possible to life outside the Aphasia Clinic. They brought in short news items, two or three paragraphs in length, to dissect and discuss. Photographs and objects, visual "cues", helped the patients to "cue into" the correct information. The patients began to make up their own sentences, writing about what they had done that day or the day before.

The therapists instructed them to pay particular attention to the five Ws–Who, What, When, Where, and Why. Kathy and the others had to be forever conscious of "keeping on track." It was so easy to forget and have bits and pieces of different thoughts find their way into the same sentence. It was like when Kathy used to go to the movies and while she was concentrating on the show, an intruding thought would pop into her mind. Back then; all she had to do was push the thought aside. It was not so easy now. In her brain Kathy's "filtering" system was not functioning properly. Intruding thoughts–perhaps sparked by the conversation of passersby or by a competing, similar memory–would fight equally for her attention. It was no wonder that at times her sentences would end up as a blending of two different thoughts. Although, as in other areas, Kathy did not experience as much of a problem with filtering as many of the other aphasics did, especially those in other groups. Some of these unfortunates, often victims of strokes, never managed to utter a single comprehensible sentence. Some, however, who could not speak, could read. Kathy could not understand this, but she was happy for whatever gains her fellow patients could make, in whatever areas.

From the ten o'clock coffee break until lunchtime, the entire unit, all twelve aphasia patients, joined together for games and activities. Sometimes they played cards, other times charades. Kathy enjoyed these times. Her laughter and friendly manner soon made her popular among the other group members.

After lunch they had "free time" from two until four o'clock. Kathy took the opportunity to break away from the routine and go to the campus health spa. Sometimes she would go to the empty room on the top floor and do her yoga. Kathy valued these private moments. She began to think about what it would be like to live on her own again. She felt she was getting closer to her goal. She could now see it within her reach, so she worked even harder.

Kathy began to wish that she had a way to express her feelings, to let others know what she had gone through and how it had affected her life. *I'll write a book,* she thought, *about myself, the accident, about how it changed my life.*

116

Then others can understand and accept me and my aphasic friends. Yes, that's exactly what she would do. She would write a book.

But it was easier said than done. She did not know where to begin. Sandy, her therapist for individual treatment, got Kathy started.

"Begin with an outline, Kathy," she said. "Write down the important dates, facts, and events. Put them in the order that they happened."

Sandy sent Kathy to the campus library. The book would become a part of Kathy's work for their one-to-one therapy sessions. The librarian helped Kathy put her memories into a logical order. Sandy helped Kathy find other resources. She helped her write letters and make phone calls.

"Before you dial the phone, Kathy," she instructed, "be sure you've written down the important questions you want to ask."

Kathy's mom had taped the first chapter of the book, *Aphasia, My World Alone,* by Helen Wulf, for Kathy. Kathy listened to the tape over and over, feeling total empathy and understanding for the author. Here was someone who *really* understood. Kathy wanted to write to Helen Wulf. Perhaps she could give Kathy some advice about writing her own book. At least she might give her moral support.

For weeks Kathy wanted to write the letter. But she could not write. She had to wait for someone to help her. Sandy was busy; she helped Kathy when she could. Kathy would just have to wait. Being dependent on others for these simple tasks angered Kathy. *The day will come when I can do these things for myself,* she fumed.

She thought about the irony of her situation. *Here I am, a college graduate who can't read,* she thought, *a social worker who has to rely on the very system she once was a part of to help her fulfill her most basic needs. My life is a paradox,* she thought. *There will always be battles for control,* Kathy thought. *I must fight again and again for*

117

control, over my body as well as my mind.

Kathy had had a "close call" during her first semester break. She had gone home to Port Clinton to visit some friends. She had been so happy; it was like old times. For a while Kathy forgot about her problems–but they did not forget her. Too much coffee, not enough sleep and forgetting to eat caught up with Kathy in a cruel way. It was four in the afternoon. Kathy was at home, lying on the couch. The last thing she remembered was walking to the bathroom early that morning. Her right arm and leg had started to shake uncontrollably. She had crawled back to the couch and collapsed there.

Now she heard someone knocking at her door.

"Want to go to a fish fry?" It was Kathy's neighbor, Janet. "Come on over to my house," she called through the screen.

"Help…, something wrong... ," Kathy stammered, her speech slurred.

Janet opened the door. "Kathy! Oh my God!" she cried.

Later, a doctor diagnosed Kathy's problem. She had had a grand mal seizure. Kathy must never again forget she had a brain injury. Her life must be governed by strict controls. She must get no less than eight hours of sleep, pay attention to nutrition, take it easy on the coffee, and take her medicine, Dilantin.

She hated medicine and she had gradually stopped taking it many months earlier. It reminded her of her restrictions. The medicine, the doctors, the restrictions caged her free spirit.

୧୦--------------------୧୨

Halloween was approaching. Kathy was excited. They were having a party! No, more than that, they were giving a party. The patients all had jobs to do. Kathy and Sarah were in charge of decorations and the menu. They hung streamers and paper skeletons on the walls. Kathy arranged a centerpiece with a pumpkin and some Indian corn. They talked about hors d'oeuvres and snack foods. Slowly and with much help, they wrote out the menu. It was great fun. Kathy had asked for help most often with her writing. She knew what she was to write, but could not think of how to spell the words.

Joy showed Kathy how to use a word division book, which breaks down commonly used words into syllables. Several words with similar first syllables were presented together. All Kathy had to do was to figure out how the word started, and she could then go down the list until she recognized the entire word. Joy worked with Kathy for many hours to help her become accustomed to sounding out the beginning letters of words.

Kathy was trying to spell "popcorn." "'P'," she started. "It starts with 'p.' P... pa... pap? P-a-p?"

"Well, almost, Kathy," Joy said trying to encourage her. "But your vowel is incorrect. Think again. *Pop*," she said, exaggerating the vowel.

"Oh? P-o-p?" Kathy asked, slowly saying the letters as she wrote them down. It helped her to think of the correct letters as she wrote them. "Yes, that's it-pop, p-o-p!"

"Great, Kathy! Yes you're right. Now, look it up in the word division book."

Kathy found 'popcorn' and 'popsicle' listed. Now she had to work on the next syllable. "Pop-c-c-corn." There was a 'c' sound and an 'r' sound in the rest of the word. It must be the p-o-p-c-o-r-n. She got it! That wasn't too bad. Spelling and writing were definitely harder for Kathy, but she was making headway. Using the word division book helped a lot.

They were starting to work with a dictionary, too. To Kathy the dictionary was mind-boggling. To break the word down into syllables was hard enough; but then how was she to find it? The words were not arranged by a common prefix, like in her word division book. The word she was hunting for was hidden somewhere among dozens of other words with the same initial letter. Kathy had to be much more accurate with her syllables when using a dictionary. It was frightening. Could she really learn to do this on her own?

Kathy's therapist helped her with other strategies for writing. They created a "cheat book" or "strategies book" that listed Kathy's most commonly missed or forgotten words. It showed prepositions with pictures, to give Kathy a visual cue. The therapist had drawn small boxes with red dots either above, below, in, out, on, or beside them. The red dot resting on the box had the word "on" written below it. The box with the dot underneath it had the words "below" or "under" written below it. There were lists of word beginnings ("dis," "un," "ex") and word endings ("est," "ed," "ing").

The therapists also helped Kathy make lists of step-by-step instructions on how to ask for phone information, cues to use in conversations, and some commonly used phrases to practice. They wrote out the numbers, one through twenty, along with the spelling of each one. Time measurements–seconds, minutes, hours, days, weeks, years–went into the strategies book also. Spelling strategies were briefly outlined: "draw a line for each syllable in the word, fill in all the letters that you know, and use phonics to sound out the rest of the letters." Kathy kept her "cheat book" with her at all times.

She was becoming more competent every day, as her phrases stretched into sentences, and sentences into paragraphs. She became more confident in conversation. Even though her speech was still deliberate and halting–the familiar "stop, wait a minute" gesture interspaced throughout–she could now maintain a train of thought and follow an idea to its conclusion. Her comprehension of what she read and heard had greatly improved, and her writing was improving, too. She began to keep a diary.

The diary renewed Kathy's interest in reading and writing. Previously, embarrassed and frustrated by her inability to read and write, Kathy had steered clear of any kind of book. One weekend, however, she had wandered into a small bookstore in downtown Ann Arbor. There she found it–a beautiful, leather bound diary, a place for special thoughts, special feelings, a place to express herself. Kathy knew immediately that the diary was meant for her.

Every evening after dinner, Kathy wrote in her diary good day, bad day, tidbits of thoughts and emotions. She began to tape again. She wanted to capture her memories and feelings, to include them in her book. The idea of writing a book became a motivating factor in Kathy's life. Through a book she could be understood, she could be accepted, she could help others. Kathy's life would have meaning beyond her own struggle once again; she would direct her energy toward helping people–helping other aphasics like herself and helping their families. It was a good goal.

She needed a new goal now that she was nearing the end of her therapy. Maybe she could even help with a support group, she thought, like they had in the hospital, but in Port Clinton, where she would soon live and work. Yes, her life could have meaning without Bill. She had proved to herself she could make it on her own. Now she had to recapture her zest for life. If there was to be more to life than just passing the time, if she was ever to have commitment, joy and vitality in her life again, Kathy knew she would have to find it for herself. And she would. Oh yes, she surely would.

℘--------------------℃

Chapter 13

LIVING FROM DAY TO DAY

"That's great, Kathy. That sentence is much better," the teacher said.

Kathy looked up at her friend and teacher, this white haired woman who had made such a difference in her life these past months since her discharge from the aphasia clinic.

"Thanks," she said. Kathy was thanking Eleanor for more than the correction of her grammar and spelling. She was thanking her for opening up a whole new dimension in her life.

Eleanor understood. God had sent Kathy to her, and she was going to do the best she could to help her. Kathy met Eleanor, an adult education teacher, when Kathy answered an ad in the Port Clinton newspaper. Kathy needed help with her reading and writing. Did Eleanor think her class would be the right place for her?

"Sure. Come on in. We'll do whatever we can," Eleanor had said.

Kathy had been working for weeks now, trying to write a letter to Helen Wulf the author of *Aphasia, My World Alone*. Kathy had finally finished the book. Her mom had taped the first and last chapters, and after many months of waiting, a church group had taped much of the rest of the book for Kathy. People always seemed willing to help, and the amount of time they invested never failed to amaze, yet frustrate her. After almost a year, she had finished the book and she wanted to communicate with this woman who had so much in common with her, to write her a letter. An impatient two-week search for Helen Wulf's address unexpectedly ended when Kathy's lawyer simply picked up the phone, called the book publisher, and got the address for her. It took five minutes, and the call could have been made two weeks earlier. Why did many tasks take so long? Why couldn't people understand how hard it was for her to be dependent on them? And then to be kept waiting, as if her needs and feelings were the lowest priority–it was enough to make her cry.

Kathy was not ungrateful. She had received so much assistance, and people were always kind. It was just the waiting that bothered her, the fact that her life had to be put on hold, that she always had to adjust to someone else's schedule. One of Kathy's greatest supporters was the librarian at her local library. Kathy had started visiting the library immediately after her return to Port Clinton. She went there to work on her reading and writing, to balance her checkbook, or to try to write letters. It was quiet and peaceful there, and at the library she was not alone. Kathy enjoyed having others around her, as long as they were not loud or distracting. Besides, here she had the librarian available to answer her questions and assist her. She came to trust him, and she treasured his friendship.

He suggested that Kathy start a chess group and have a chess tournament. He knew that Kathy loved chess. He thought it would help her meet people and become more confident. So Kathy faced the challenge of organizing and scheduling an event for the first time outside the hospital setting. It took all of her concentration and effort and lots of help from her friend, but she did it. The tournament lasted eight weeks. Kathy had a great time, and she felt very pleased with herself.

Kathy realized that she must continue to work on her problem areas–speaking, reading, and writing–and that she still needed the support of others who knew and understood her condition. She was out of the hospital, done with therapy, and on her own. But she was not done working. She would never be done.

There was a head injury support group at a rehabilitation center in Green Springs, Ohio, about an hour's drive from

Port Clinton. Kathy joined the group and went to the monthly meetings. It made her feel less isolated, and there she was able to support other head injury patients like herself, many of whom had not come as far as she had. In Green Springs the thought of having her own support group began to grow in her mind. Kathy felt very alive and so much more in control of her life when she was able to help others. She wanted to do more.

It was not long before an opportunity to help someone else came to Kathy. A family in Port Clinton had experienced a tragedy. A young man, the son of a woman Kathy knew, had been in a car accident. Jim was in a coma. Kathy went to the mother and asked what she could do to help.

The mother had been driving the two-hour round trip to the hospital everyday to visit her son. She did not want him to be alone. Perhaps Kathy could visit him sometime, so that she could take a break. Kathy arranged to visit Jim once a week. She went once a week for four months. She talked to Jim, told him of her own struggle and success. She encouraged him to try, to never give up. Although Jim rarely showed any sign of being conscious, Kathy just kept on talking.

At Christmas Kathy brought Jim a gift–a plaque. She read him the inscription: "Do what you can, where you are, with what you have." Jim, who had shown few signs of conscious understanding since his accident, finally responded. Just as Kathy finished reading the inscription, tears began to roll down Jim's cheeks. Kathy rushed to tell the nurse, who was elated. This was a wonderful sign. Kathy felt deep joy.

"You're going to make it, Jim," she promised him.

After this visit Kathy had gone back to Missouri to spend the holidays with her family. Six weeks later, upon returning to Port Clinton, she found that Jim had come out of the coma. *Now the real work begins,* she thought.

Kathy thought it was time to do something about

starting a support group in Port Clinton. She had been going to Green Springs for almost a year, participating in the support group there. She had "learned the ropes." Now, along with Josephine, Jim's mother, Kathy began to organize a support group in Port Clinton. They sent letters to doctors, therapists, and the local newspaper, letting people know that there soon would be a place for victims of strokes and head injuries to get together and support one another.

Kathy was a little frightened by the prospect of starting a support group. She and Josephine would have to act as "leaders." The others would look to them for guidance. Was she ready for this?

One day the social worker at the Green Springs Rehabilitation Center called Kathy and asked her to speak at the next group meeting, to tell her story in her own words. Kathy decided it would give her experience for her own group and would give her confidence. But Kathy was terrified. She had not talked in front of a group since her therapy sessions. Her speech was still not good. What if they couldn't understand her? The social worker finally persuaded her to do it, but Kathy was sure she would make a fool of herself. *Oh well, it won't be the first time,* she thought.

The night before the speech, Kathy was lying on the couch, worrying about it. Suddenly an idea popped into her head–call dial-a-prayer. Why not? She had not been what you would call a devout Catholic, but Kathy believed in the power of prayer, especially since the accident. She often thought of her "mystical experience." Since that day she had not felt the same closeness, that very real presence of God in her life, but she hoped that it would happen again. She picked up the phone. The message was uplifting, encouraging. Kathy felt herself relax. A peacefulness came over her, and she went to bed, feeling much more confident.

The next day, she talked to the group, just trying to be herself. She made mistakes. She faltered, stopped and started over. No one seemed to notice. But they did notice what she said. Others had given up on her, labeled her a lost cause, but she had overcome not only the physical disabilities, but the skepticism of others. She had proved them wrong. She did it because she wanted it very much. She would not accept defeat. This kind of perseverance was what it took.

As she looked out over the audience, Kathy saw a tiny glimmer of hope in the eyes of a few of the patients. They could do it, she promised them, if they tried hard enough. She was proof that they should never stop trying.

During this year (mid-1983 to mid-1984), Kathy was working with Eleanor. They had worked for four weeks on her letter to Helen Wulf. Kathy's writing was almost incoherent. She used the wrong words, transposed her nouns and pronouns, and wrote the opposite of what she had meant to say. Eleanor, who knew Kathy, was the only one who could "translate" her messages.

Eleanor was infinitely patient with Kathy. She was a woman of deep faith. She had worked with lost causes and the mentally deficient. There was not much she had not seen. But Eleanor saw great potential in Kathy, hidden deep within a confused mind. Kathy needed two things–patience and faith. Eleanor had both to give.

Eleanor could not bring herself to tell Kathy how poorly she was writing. Instead she found whatever she could to praise in Kathy's work. Writing was Kathy's weakest point, but sentence-by-sentence Eleanor gently guided Kathy to make changes, to rearrange and rethink her words. All the while she praised Kathy's determination, her effort. As Kathy's confidence grew, she seemed to write a little better, too.

Finally, after four weeks of hard work, Kathy had completed the letter to Helen Wulf. It was a milestone for Kathy–her first written letter in four years.

Helen Wulf answered Kathy's letter within the week. Kathy was elated. She was certain Helen understood her. Only a person who had traveled the same path could understand how much this prompt reply meant to Kathy, how much it validated her efforts. Helen had written an encouraging, hopeful letter. She was thrilled with Kathy's success. Would Kathy share her story with Helen's support group in her newsletter, "A Stroke of Luck"?

Kathy did not know what to say. It had been so hard to write the first letter to Helen. It had cost her four weeks of her life. Could she write an article? Was she willing to put out that much effort all over again?

I guess that's what it's all about now, Kathy thought to herself. *Either keep forging ahead or call it quits right here and now. Okay, I'll do it,* she decided.

Kathy started all over again, writing another letter, this time to the hundreds of stroke and head injury patients who looked to "A Stroke of Luck" to uplift and inspire them. Kathy knew she had no choice. Her life's direction had been set.

As Kathy and Eleanor began to work on the article, Eleanor encouraged Kathy to look inside herself for strength. She knew writing the first letter had taken a lot out of Kathy. She saw the pain on Kathy's face as she fought to overcome the feelings of despair that could only be expected when facing such an enormous task. Kathy knew the job would have taken her hours at the most before the accident. Now it would take her weeks, even months, to accomplish. This thought almost devastated her. But she hoped that this time it would be easier. Kathy always hoped for the best. She tried to keep her sights on the positive.

One day Eleanor invited Kathy to come to her prayer group. Eleanor's prayer group was the other part of her life's work. Through it she had helped heal much suffering. Eleanor seemed to have a special touch. Those who knew her felt the power that she could bring forth when she tuned into herself and prayed. It was almost physical.

"I don't know much about praying," Kathy admitted to the group. "I haven't done it for a while."

"That's okay," one of the women assured her. "We'll teach you the same way that our Lord taught his disciples.

Just repeat after me. Our Father, who art in Heaven...

As Kathy prayed, she added a message of her own. "Remember me, God. It's Kathy. We met once before."

Kathy felt a trembling deep inside her as she spoke these words. Tears came to her eyes. *He does remember,* she thought. *He hasn't forgotten me.* She knew she had found a new source of strength, a friend, who would not forsake her, even in her bleakest hour.

Kathy became a regular member of Eleanor's prayer group. She wanted to hold on to what she had found. Shortly after she joined the group, Kathy approached Eleanor.

"I've had my first revelation," Kathy said. "It's a miracle that I'm alive." She spoke the words quietly. Her eyes were intense, and tears brimmed over the edges.

"Why, Kathy, we all knew that," Eleanor replied, stunned at Kathy's intensity in relating such an obvious fact.

"Yes, I know," said Kathy. "You knew, but I didn't. God had to tell me."

Kathy began to listen for God's voice in her silent meditations. She hoped to renew the two-way communication she had experienced during the "dream" after the accident. So far she had had several messages— voices in her mind that were so quiet, so peaceful, so *certain* that she knew it must be his voice. Yet when she had tried to respond, she had lost the feeling. She wanted to regain that wonderful experience of *being there* with God, talking one to one, person to person. *Perhaps that happens only once in a lifetime,* she thought. Maybe she could never reopen that pathway. But she would try.

One night Kathy went with a friend to hear a speaker on the topic, "Learn How To Pray." The speaker, a nun, told the group, "You can pray to Jesus, to the angels, or you can just talk to the God in your heart."

The God in my heart, thought Kathy. *That's it. If I talk to the God in my heart, then he will hear me. I know he will.*

Kathy went home, feeling serene and peaceful. Getting ready for bed, combing out her hair, she was startled by the sounds of music. Her music box had started to play, all on its own. I know, Kathy thought, *I'm not alone.* She smiled and went to bed.

Working on the article for "A Stroke Of Luck" was difficult for Kathy, but it provided its own rewards. The article was about coping in everyday life as an aphasic. Thinking about what she would include in the article forced Kathy to look at her life and pinpoint her own strategies. She scrutinized her habits. She had learned to control consciously many unconscious patterns. Her control over situations had improved. Kathy had never been shy or embarrassed about what she had had to do to function in the real world. "When eating out," she wrote in the article, "I use lots and lots of napkins."

After six weeks of intense work, Kathy submitted her article to "A Stroke Of Luck." Helen Wulf printed it as it was, unedited. Kathy was overcome with pride when she read it.

Kathy had been attending the prayer group with Eleanor for about a month. Eleanor was praying daily for Kathy. She had become quite attached to Kathy. She wanted so much to help her, to see Kathy lead a normal life. But, as one who becomes accustomed to another's habits, Eleanor had stopped noticing Kathy's constant stumblings, her "Stop, wait a minute" gesture. These gestures, along with Kathy's other communication problems, were so familiar to Eleanor that they had become just another part of Kathy's demeanor. They endeared Kathy to Eleanor even more.

One day, however, it occurred to Eleanor that something seemed different about Kathy. Eleanor had known Kathy for over a year. They had been in the prayer group together for a little over a month. She was sure that whatever it was, it had happened suddenly, during the past week. She kept a close watch on Kathy that day. To her surprise, Eleanor noted that the familiar "stop, wait a minute" gesture was almost absent. Her speech was more clear and precise than Eleanor had ever heard it. There was a definite, dramatic improvement in Kathy's use of words, her grammar, and her speech patterns. It was as if overnight Kathy had made a quantum leap in her ability to communicate. Eleanor smiled. She knew why this had happened. It was not just the year of work. That had helped of course. But this–this *sudden* improvement could only be the work of one person. *Thank you,* Eleanor silently said. *Thank you, thank you, thank you.*

ℰℴ--------------------ℭℛ

Kathy was waiting for some response to her advertisements about the support group. She began to wonder if the group would ever get off the ground. Maybe it was too much for her to tackle?

Aside from the support group, other concerns were on Kathy's mind. She was trying to work on her book, but it was not going well. She had her tapes from therapy and her diary. But as she listened to the tapes, she was so overcome with depression that she could not think coherently. She felt she was being swallowed up by self-pity. And she was lonely. She missed having a man in her life. There was one man, a friend, but Kathy missed the romance, the excitement of having "a real boyfriend."

Then, unexpectedly, Kathy received a terrible blow. Her new friend, Glen, the only man in her life, died suddenly. He had been so young, so vital, in his early forties, not much older than Kathy herself. Kathy felt as if the rug had been pulled out from under her. Her confidence was shattered; her faith was shaken. How could this happen? He had been her friend. She had counted on him. Now he was gone.

All of Kathy's insecurities and fears seemed to rush over her. What security did she have left in life now, she who knew first hand just how precarious life was? There were no guarantees–not for life, not for friendship–no guarantees that some day there would be someone for her.

Kathy felt abandoned, alone, and frightened. *How can I deal with all this tragedy?* she wondered. *Will I really be able to make something of my life?*

Kathy crawled into bed and cried herself to sleep. At 6:00 A.M. she was awakened suddenly. What was it? She strained her ears, listening for a noise, whatever it was that had caused her to sit bolt upright in her bed. But she heard nothing. There was only silence. Then, deep inside her mind, Kathy felt a stirring, an opening. A familiar voice rang out.

"Kathy, start a support group. Finish your book. And I will take care of the rest."

"It's you. It's really you, isn't it?" Kathy whispered into the darkness. A peacefulness, a quiet serenity came over her like a warm blanket. She laid her head back onto the pillow and slept like a baby.

Later that morning, Kathy woke up with a new attitude. She felt the presence, the peace, the gift of love from the previous night still within her. *I have a partner,* she thought, *and a plan. Now I have to really get to work.* Kathy threw herself with renewed interest into writing her book. Working diligently, she outlined dates, events, and important ideas that she wanted to recount. A friend typed a manuscript of approximately sixty pages from Kathy's taped notes. She had her "first draft." But she wanted it to be more than a memoir, more than a diary. Kathy wanted her book to be a story that would be read not only by aphasics and their families, but by others as well. She wanted to build a wider understanding and acceptance of herself and others like her among people not already involved with head injury victims. Maybe she needed an assistant, "a ghost writer." She would think about it. The right answer would come to her.

Kathy had always relied on her intuition. She used it to guide her, to tell her her real feelings. She knew now that this intuition was a part of the "God in her heart" that the nun had talked about, and she was now even more determined to listen to it. Kathy knew that if she followed her heart, everything would be taken care of, just as she had been promised.

Kathy's life, like her speech, began to improve suddenly. A sense of purpose pervaded everything she did. She finally knew why her life had been spared. She was part of a plan, and she intended to fulfill her role to the best of her abilities. During the next year, Kathy's support group grew. Jim was able to join her now, and there was another lady, as well. They went out to dinner; they talked; they went to lectures to learn how to cope. Through Helen Wulf's newsletter, Kathy became pen pal for a stroke victim. His letters inspired and uplifted her. He always had something nice or funny to say. Fred, her pen pal, was also writing a book. They exchanged notes on the ups and downs of being an author.

In 1986 Kathy's support group added a member, and Kathy gained a friend, as well. Faith, Kathy's friend, was an accident victim like Kathy, but she had no problems with her speech. In fact, she loved to talk. Kathy was delighted. They hit it off immediately.

Kathy finally felt at peace in her life. She knew that whatever her life brought, she was in charge now. By following her heart, she could never go wrong.

As Kathy dressed to catch the flight to Kerriville, Texas, she thought back over the last seven years of her life. They had certainly been challenging and not at all what she had expected. But now, here she stood getting ready to meet her pen pal, Fred, and her mentor, Helen Wulf, at the National Aphasia Conference in Kerriville, where Kathy would speak to hundreds of doctors and therapists. She decided that she would not want her life to have gone any other way. *I've grown so much,* she thought. *I think I've become a better person. My life has purpose, meaning beyond myself. I feel that I'm no longer alone.*

132

As Kathy smiled at her reflection in the mirror, the light, melodious tones of a music box drifted through the room.

℘)---------------------Cℛ

Epilogue

Kathy's life has seen many changes since she completed the book in 1990. She continues to focus on her work and the joy of life, despite some personal losses. Shortly following the completion of the book, Kathy and Bill had a son. Considering the head injury, the idea of having a child after the accident seemed like a dream to her. This dream was realized and Jonathan brings tremendous joy and purpose to Kathy's life.

In 1994, Kathy moved from Ohio back to her hometown of St. Louis. She felt she needed a fresh start and to be near her father who was suffering from cancer. She settled into a comfortable house near her parents and focused on raising Jonathan. Kathy maintained a friendship with Bill until his untimely death at the age of 53. "I always loved Bill," she admitted. "He was never completely out of the picture. We had an off and on relationship for 25 years."

Kathy has recovered to the point that most people who meet her are unaware of her aphasia and her disability. She has limited use of her right hand, but is self-sufficient. Occasionally, Kathy will hesitate while speaking, in search of the right words. "If I can't say a word, I just use another word, she said. "It is not a life or death situation."

Kathy is in demand as a speaker at rehabilitation centers, colleges, and conferences, where she shares her inspirational story. She is also involved in spreading the word about aphasia with the intent of educating, and helping as many people as she can reach. In addition to her community involvement, Kathy continues to pursue several personal interests. She stays active in two singles groups in hope of finding a new relationship. She is active in the Catholic Church, and she is involved in issues concerning the disabled in her community.

Kathy is deeply appreciative of her second chance at

life and eagerly seeks out new experiences. Life should be filled with fun, love, and peace. In her own words, "Life is what you make it and you have to roll with the punches."

Jean Abernathy
St. Louis, MO

Appendix

I. GLOSSARY OF TERMS

aphasia: impairment, due to brain damage, of the ability to interpret and formulate language symbols; a loss of, or reduction in, the capacity to decode linguistic elements. The degree of impairment is proportionate to the decrease in intellectual function. Aphasia involves difficulties both in the comprehension of language and in its formulation and expression, in auditory comprehension, reading, speaking, and writing. It usually involves injury to the left hemisphere of the brain, which is responsible for language functions.

apraxia: an articulation disorder resulting from impairment (e.g., as a result of brain damage) of the ability to control the muscles and the sequencing of muscle movement needed for any activity, including volitional speech; it is not the result of weakening of the muscles.

dysarthria: a disorder in the articulation of speech due to the loss of motor skills. It is characterized by the substitution, omission, addition, and distortions of speech sounds. There may be a change of speed in the speech or a slurring of words.

PICA: Porch Index of Communicative Ability, a test to determine the degree of language disturbance in an aphasic person. The PICA test was published by Bruce Porch in 1967.

II. APHASIA SEVERITY RATING SCALE

0. No useful ability to speak and no comprehension of auditory messages.

1. Fragmentary comprehension: questioning, guessing, limited exchange of information in conversation; the listener carries the burden of conversation.

2. The patient can talk about familiar subjects with help from the listener; the patient frequently fails to convey message but does share in the burden of conversation.

3. The patient can discuss almost all everyday problems with little or no assistance, but the reduction of speech and/or comprehension makes it almost impossible for the patient to discuss certain topics.

4. Some obvious loss of fluency in speech of facility of comprehension, but without significant limitation of the ideas expressed or the forms of expression.

5. Minimal discernible impairment of speech, but the patient may have subjective difficulties that are not apparent to listener.

In 1985 a support group was organized in the area. Here is our brochure.

HEAD TRAUMA SUPPORT GROUP:
PEOPLE HELPING PEOPLE

Sharing is the art of living,
Living is the art of loving,
Loving is the art of caring,
Caring is the art of sharing,

Our Purpose

We are a social club for recovering head trauma patients, their spouses, extended families and friends. Our volunteers' primary objectives are to create a comfortable environment aiming towards keeping members from becoming reclusive. Here they can relax among others who are making similar adjustments into the main stream of their communities. The Head Trauma Support Group provides opportunities to share experiences and make new friends.

Our Goals

Identify personal desires, needs, and perception of self to others and their problems. Keep participants up-dated on new information related to their community and their interaction with it. Community awareness and the acceptance of the rehabilitation process.

The Family

Active participation of all family members is encouraged in order to provide an emotional supportive environment. Learning and understanding head trauma, stroke, and their effects. Group discussions and sharing experiences with other families.

Membership

Membership is open to persons recovering from head trauma, strokes, their families and to others actively interested in promoting their interests.

Head Trauma Support Group, People Helping People, can benefit you if you have experienced any of the following:

- Loss of Memory
- Disruption in logic and judgment
- Loss of consciousness or coma
- Feelings that nobody understands what you are going through
- Feelings of frustration or helplessness in coping with spouse, child, or friend with head trauma.
- A need to have a place you can say what you feel and be who you are.

Since 1985, a new organization Traumatic Brain Injury-TBI has been established all over the country. It was chartered in 1981 and strives though regional chapters to improve the quality of life for people with brain injuries.

Anybody can start a support group–just people who are friends; all they need is a location, a date, and a time.

Kathy's Articles

FROM KATHY OF PORT CLINTON, OHIO

(Reprinted from "A Stroke Of Luck", Vol. 2, No. 2, April 1985)

I am writing an article because I know that many people have had head injuries. The victims need a support group–happy, sad, frustrated or deep in thought. We need each other to channel our lives to reach God's power. Life is what you make it. You have to "roll with the punches."

I had an auto accident 5 years ago and it's changed my life, hopefully for the better. I was a social worker and on the side I tended bar, just for kicks. Now I am really busy coping with aphasia.

The dictionary says: "Aphasia, trouble with communications, loss of speech." Everybody is different in aphasia. My right hand and right foot have no feeling. I went to physical therapy, occupational therapy, language disorder and speech therapy for 2 ½ years daily. I am still working at therapy independently–making lists, balancing my check book, going to the store, and just getting dressed and looking presentable. That's a chore!

Everybody has ups and downs, good days and bad days, but head injured victims are a lot more intense and sensitive. I know because the left side of my brain is damaged. Many days I can't communicate so I call a friend just to check if my speech is OK or not. If my speech is all jumbled up I have 2 choices: stay at home, or go out and function in public. The Key is a positive attitude.

You have to gain self-confidence and I am learning every day. I have to psyche myself up and work at relaxing. (Yoga is a great "calmer downer.") Accept yourself, put yourself forward and enjoy. If my speech is awful I don't worry about it, "grin and bear it" and tomorrow is a new day.

I am grateful to share with you some of my helpful hints in aphasia. Talking Books are great. I got an application from the Public Library for "Blind and Physically Handicapped" assistance. It required my doctor's signature and I received a tape recorder, record player and a catalog.

I have received lots of tapes. I sent several tapes back which I could not comprehend—novels had too many characters, cities and scenery. It was mind-boggling. I like true stories, relaxation methods, psychology and spiritual readings. They are uplifting. I receive "Good Housekeeping" magazine on records. It's great because I clean my house and listen. If I have a good article I listen well or tape it.

I read the newspaper daily. It's a small paper so I know the names and skim it. If the paper has an important article I cut it out and later friends read it to me. Close friends read the letters, important bills and paper clippings.

You have to have major and minor goals with a purpose for living. My Big Goals are: working at my book, forming a support group in the county and learning to be a professional pool shark. With Little Goals I make a list for the week: cleaning house, going to the Laundromat, making phone calls, writing letters, paying bills, and when I finish each chore I check it off.

I have my own tape recorder and it's super! I tape letters to family or friends. If I watch TV such as Talk Shows or a good movie I will tape it and enjoy it again. Don't buy cheap tapes because they break easily. Buy name brands on sale about $2 a box.

Now I'm living alone and I like to be as independent as possible. My right hand, foot and face have no sensation. In the winter I wear gloves or mittens so I won't get frostbite.

Make-up and lipstick are a good camouflage; I hold my hand as natural as possible; paint my fingernails on my right hand and my friend paints my left hand. If not, I paint it and wait until it dries. It takes a half hour. Patience is a Virtue!

141

A plastic curling iron is great. One time I curled my hair and burned my hand badly with a metal iron. I don't like to use long sleeved shirts with buttons. If the cuff is loose I keep it buttoned, wash it still buttoned.

In the summer I wear thongs and in the winter I wear boots or slip-on shoes. Some handicapped people use special shoelaces, but I don't, it's too much trouble. Velcro tennis shoes are super!

For women–if you wear a bra, snap it and slip the bra on and never unsnap again even when washing. When shaving your underarms an electric razor is best. Don't cut yourself.

For an important phone call–write a list before you call and then practice talking before you call. Be cheerful but if it's a bad day, wait until you can be positive.

I like to plan what to wear before I go to bed at night because it's difficult to get up in the morning and function. Get a calculator! I like to go to the Library, it's quiet and I pay bills or write letters and enjoy the people. The librarian helps me spell words. With a fixed pencil sharpener I switch hands.

If I am in a restaurant or Lounge and it's noisy and there is loud music, I have learned to block it out. I calm down, relax and listen to the people jabber. I can't understand jokes; I laugh but don't get them too fast.

Now I have a driver's license but I have 2 restrictions: 1-automatic drive and 2-spin knob/power steering (right hand). Personally I love to ride my bicycle.

Nutrition is really important. Four years ago I had a seizure because I forgot to eat, I drank beer, had little sleep and I had 6 cups of coffee. Now I take Dilantin to prevent seizures, I drink decaffeinated coffee, eat nutritious meals and I like to sleep at least 6 hours. In table manners, I have to have a lot of napkins; in buffet style other friends help me or I make 2 or 3 trips. I worry about dropping my plate. A new gadget has a plate with a glass holder.

My old teacher made a notebook like numbers,

grammar, verb tenses, pronouns (he and she group, ugh!) and spelling strategies. I use a pocket dictionary and check because many times I am forgetful. I mark the word if I use it frequently. My sister gave me "Speak and Spell" (Texas Instruments) and it is super because I can do it alone and it's fun. I have a card which is given to senior citizens and permanently disabled for discounts at certain stores and restaurants like Ben Franklin or McDonalds.

Aphasics are slow but sure. I worked on the "Stroke of Luck" article for 6 weeks because writing, spelling and comprehension are not what they used to be since these abilities were lost. The ticket for success is self-confidence and a good mental attitude. Be good to yourself. Listen to the music and take time to smell the flowers.

Kathy Hughes
745 Bergerac Drive
St. Louis, MO 63141
khughesj@aol.com

AN INSIDE VIEW OF APHASIA

(Reprinted from "Prevention", Vol. 37, No. 7, July 1985)

I had an auto accident five years ago and thus became a victim of aphasia [injury or disease of the brain causing loss of ability to communicate in speech or writing]. And I wanted people to know what life was like from an aphasic's point of view.

Since my accident my right hand, right foot and right side of my face have had no feeling. Daily, I went to physical therapy, occupational therapy and language therapy for 2½ years. And I am still working at therapy independently, practicing making lists, balancing my checkbook, going to the store, and just getting dressed and looking presentable. These are all extremely simple tasks, but for me they're a chore.

Many days I have trouble talking, so I call a friend to check if my speech is understandable. If my speech is all jumbled up, I have two choices: stay at home or go out and function in public.

The key is a positive attitude. I have to gain self-confidence, and I'm learning every day. I have to psyche myself up, and really work at relaxing. I have to accept myself. If my speech is awful, I don't worry about it. I just grin and bear it, knowing that tomorrow is a new day.

I have to have a purpose for living–some major and minor goals. My big goals are writing a book, forming a support group for aphasics–and learning to be a professional pool shark. My little goals are cleaning house, going to the Laundromat, making phone calls, writing letters and paying bills.

Since I have no feeling in my right hand, in the winter I'm sure to wear gloves or mittens so I don't get frostbitten. Makeup and lipstick are good camouflage for the side of my face that has no feeling. I hold my hand as steady as possible and paint my fingernails on my right hand; my friend paints my left hand. If my friend isn't available, I paint it myself–a half-hour job. Patience is a virtue. I keep the cuffs of my shirts buttoned (too hard to button and unbutton) and even wash them that way.

Before making an important phone call I write a list of conversation topics before calling and then practice talking. Before I go to bed I plan what I'll wear the next day because it's difficult to get up in the morning and function. I use a calculator. If I'm in a noisy restaurant I have to block out the sounds–too confusing. When people tell me jokes, I laugh but I don't get the humor–the words come too fast.

Aphasic's are slow but sure. I worked on this letter for six weeks because writing, spelling and comprehension are now extremely difficult for me. But I know the ticket for success is self-confidence and a good mental attitude. I listen to the music and take time to smell the flowers.

Kathy Hughes
Port Clinton, Ohio

MY SUMMER EXPERIENCE *Kathy Hughes*

(Reprinted from "A Stroke Of Luck", Vol. 2, No. 2, April 1986)

Did you ever have too many irons in the fire? I did last spring. I was working on my book, starting a Head Trauma Support Group and very busy with all that entails.., writing letters, going to meetings, calling people, etc., and had very little rest.

I felt I needed to meet new and interesting people, so I made reservations for 6 weeks on Put-In-Bay, an island on Lake Erie. God's Country. I bought a small but adequate trailer.

The first problem I had to face was getting the trailer to the Island. I did not have a hitch and everybody claimed to be too busy to pull the trailer to the ferry. Eventually, my sister Nancy drove 100 miles from Madison, OH, a suburb of Cleveland, to Port Clinton and towed my trailer to the ferry.

I am a novice camper but I learned a lot about water and propane hook-ups, leveling the trailer and setting up camp with my sister. We were so proud of ourselves we stayed up late celebrating. The next morning Nancy went back home.

I knew two families on the Island and in the process of getting organized I met some new friends, the owner of the campground and his wife and 2 daughters. We became good friends. These families were my Island support system.

In spite of them I felt alone although I was surrounded by campers. I love nature, and with my bicycle, my trailer and my inflatable dinghy I felt closer to God. After all, Put-In-Bay is His country and I am on it!

Early in the morning with the birds chirping at the sunrise, I get up and visit the shower rooms and brush my teeth. I return to the trailer and make coffee. Simple tasks are chores for me without help, but I gain independence doing for myself.

I ride my bicycle around the Island and attend lectures at the Perry International Peace Monument. I also visit caves on the Island, which were once used as prisons. I gained a little knowledge of history. I sampled the nationally known products of the local winery.

My campsite is 1 mile from Put-In-Bay. That's where the action is. There is miniature golf, a departure point for railroad tours, a go-cart rental and lots of shops and restaurants, plus an active Marina with beautiful yachts.

There are many happy people about the town. They play pool and chess, catch fish, clean fish, watch the sunset and populate the bars and restaurants. The bars and restaurants have lots of live entertainment. Some serve pizza, some serve barbecue chicken, some sell only ice cream. My cup of tea is to ride my bike to the ice cream stand, buy an ice cream cone and watch the sun set. I gained 10 pounds!

There are also plenty of drunks about. They don't know how to relax and have fun so they drink and raise Cain. I was a kid once but I'm not anymore. A lot of people who are in their 40's and above are in town and still acting like kids, so I ride my bike back to the camp. This is why I like the weekdays but not the weekends. The campers are happy, outgoing folk. At night we light a big fire, eat popcorn and talk about the 'good old days.' I learned a lot on Put-In-Bay.

In August my family vacationed for 3 weeks near Port Clinton, OH. I stayed at the family cottage. It was a bad month for me because the transition is hard for me. I had 3 houses: my house, my parents cottage and my trailer. I felt lost.

My parents have 12 children and my brothers and sisters have children. I love my family but I can't cope with crowds. It is very difficult for an individual with aphasia to converse with 22 people.

I was depressed due to one major and a lot of minor problems. I prayed a lot. In September, God answered my prayers. I lost the man in my life... a man who caused me problem after depressing problem. Now I feel free. I am very busy and very fulfilled. And I lost those 10 pounds!

I go to adult basic education twice a week and I'm working again on the Head Trauma Support Group. We have had 2 successful meetings so far and another is planned for next month. I also find time to relax and shoot pool. This had been a great month.

I learned a lot this summer about people and myself. It was an adventurous experience and I grew with it. The needs of those who suffer from aphasia are different but we all need perseverance. When you have aphasia you have to be willing to stick with it. It takes strength and courage not to give up when you know what you are trying to say but the words will not come out right.

But do you know what? Five years ago one doctor said I would never speak or write again. So if you know someone who is aphasic, keep hanging in there and keep praying... but do take time to smell the flowers.

Brain Injury Association States

Go to http://www.biausa.org/stateoffices.htm for the latest updates to association information.

BIA of Arizona
President: Mary Bradley
Executive Director: Mattie Cummins
777 E. Missouri Avenue, Suite 101
Phoenix, AZ 85014
Phone: 602-508-8024
Infoline: 602-323-9165
Toll Free: 888-500-9165
Fax: 602-508-8285
E-mail: info@biaaz.org
Website: www.biaaz.org

BIA of Arkansas
President: Dianne Gutierrez
PO Box 26236
Little Rock, AR 72221-6236
Phone: (501) 374-3585
In State: (800) 235-2443
Fax: (501) 918-6595
E-mail: info@brainassociation.org
Website: http://www.brainassociation.org

BIA of California
President: Mark Ashley
Administrative Assistant: Paula Daoutis
2658 Mt. Vernon Ave.
Bakersfield, CA 93306
Phone: 661-872-4903
Fax: 661-873-2508
E-mail: calbiainfo@yahoo.com
Website: www.calbia.org

BIA of Colorado
President: Daniel Sloane, Esq.
Exec Director: J. Paul Price
4200 West Conejos Place # 524
Denver, CO 80204
Phone: 303-355-9969
In State: 800-955-2443
Fax: 303-355-9968
E-mail: informationreferral@biacolorado.org
Website: www.biacolorado.org

BIA of Connecticut
President of the Board: Charles Lyons
Program Director: Julie Peters
333 East River Drive, Suite 106
East Hartford, CT 06108
Phone: 860-721-8111
In State: 800-278-8242
Fax: 860-721-9008
E-mail: general@biact.org
Website: www.biact.org

BIA of Delaware
President: John Goodier
Executive Director: James A. Burcham
Brain Injury Association of Delaware, Inc.
32 West Loockerman Street, Suite 103
Dover, DE 19904
Toll Free: (800) 411-0505
Fax: (302) 678-3183 (*call first*)
E-mail: biadresourcecenter@cavtel.net
Website: www.biausa.org/Delaware/bia.htm

BIA of Florida
President: Bernard Brucker, Ph.D., ABPP
Exec Director: Valerie E. Breen M.S.S.A., ACSW
Admin Secretary: Rose Ledbetter
1621 Metropolitan Boulevard, Suite B
Tallahassee, FL 32308
Phone: 850-410-0103
In State: 800-992-3442
Fax: 850-410-0105
E-mail: biaftalla@biaf.org
Website: www.biaf.org

BIA of Georgia
Director: Karen Parsley.
Center for Rehab Medicine
1441 Clifton Rd. NE #114-A
Atlanta, GA 30322
Phone: 404-712-5504
Fax: 404-712-0463
Website: http://www.braininjurygeorgia.org

BIA of Hawaii
President: Mary Isley-Wilson
2201 Waimano Home Road, Hale E
Pearl City, HI 96782-1474
Phone: 808-454-0699
Fax: 808-454-1975
E-mail: biahi@verizon.net
Website: www.biausa.org/Hawaii

BIA of Idaho
President: Michelle Featherston
P.O Box 414
Boise, ID 83701-0414
Phone: 208-342-0999
In State: 888-374-3447
Fax: 208-333-0026
E-mail: info@biaid.org
Website: www.biaid.org

BIA of Illinois
President: Ginny Lazzara
Exec Director: Philicia Deckard
P.O. Box 64420
Chicago, IL 60664-0420
Phone: 312-726-5699
Toll Free: 800-699-6443
Fax: 312-630-4011
E-mail: info@biail.org
Website: www.biail.org

BIA of Indiana
Exec Director: Stacy Payne
9531 Valparaiso Court, Suite A
Indianapolis, IN 46268
Phone: 317-356-7722
Fax: 317-808-7770
E-mail: info@biai.org
Website: www.biausa.org/Indiana

BIA of Iowa
President: Julie Dixon
Exec Director: Geoffrey Lauer
317 East Sixth Street
Des Moines, IA 50309-1903
Phone: 515-244-5606
Toll free: 800-444-6443
Fax: 800-381-0812
E-mail: info@biaia.org
Website : www.biaia.org

BIA of Kansas and Greater Kansas City
Board President: Dave Banks
Exec Director: Betsy Johnson
P.O. Box 413072
Kansas City, MO 64105
Phone: 816-842-8607
In State: 800-783-1356
Fax: 816-842-1531
E-mail: Lliggett@biaks.org
Website: www.biaks.org

BIA of Kentucky
President: Chell Austin
Exec Director: Melinda Mast
7410 New LaGrange Rd. Suite 100
Louisville, KY 40222
Phone: 502-493-0609
In State: 800-592-1117 x223
Fax: 502-426-2993
Website: www.biak.us

BIA of Maine
President: Mary Lombardo
Contact Person: Leslie DuVall
13 Washington Street
Waterville, ME 04901
Phone: 207-861-9900
In State: 800-275-1233
Fax: 207-861-4617
E-mail: info@biame.org
Website: www.biame.org

BIA of Maryland
President: Patricia Janus
Exec Director: Diane Tripplet - triplett@biamd.org
2200 Kernan Drive
Baltimore, MD 21207
Phone: 410-448-2924
In State: 800-221-6443
Fax: 410-448-3541
E-mail: info@biamd.org
Website: www.biamd.org

BIA of Massachusetts
President: Gregory L. Zagloba
Exec Director: Arlene Korab
30 Lyman St.
Westborough, MA 01581
Phone: 508-475-0032
In State: 800-242-0030
Fax: 508-475-0400
E-mail: biama@biama.org
Website: www.biama.org

BIA of Michigan
Chair: William Buccalo
President: Michael F. Dabbs
**Director of Programs
and Services:** Cheryl A. Burda
7305 Grand River, Suite 100
Brighton, MI 48114-7379
Phone: 810-229-5880
In State: 800-772-4323
Fax: 810-229-8947
E-mail: info@biami.org
Website: www.biami.org

BIA of Minnesota
Chair: Terri Traudt
Exec Director: Ardis Sandstrom
34 13th Avenue NE, Suite B001
Minneapolis, MN 55413
Phone: 612-378-2742
In State: 800-669-6442
Fax: 612-378-2789
E-mail: info@braininjurymn.org
Website: www.braininjurymn.org

BIA of Mississippi
President and Chair: Howard Katz, Ph.D.
Exec Director: Lee Jenkens
P.O Box 55912
Jackson, MS 39296-5912
Phone: 601-981-1021
In State: 800-641-6442
Fax: 601-981-1039
E-mail: biaofms@aol.com
Website: www.members.aol.com/biaofms/index.htm

BIA of Missouri
President: Lynne Unnerstall
Exec Director: Scott Gee
10270 Page Ave, Suite 100
St. Louis, MO 63132
Phone: 314-426-4024
Fax: 314-426-3290
In State: 800-377-6442 (MO, IL, KS only)
E-mail: info@biamo.org
Website: www.biamo.org

BIA of Montana
Co-Presidents: Anita Roessman
and Brenda Toner
Staff: Kristn Morgan
1280 S. 3rd St. West, Suite 4
Missoula, MT 59802
Phone: 406-541-6442
In State: 800-241-6442
E-mail: biam@biamt.org
Website: www.biamt.org

BIA of New Hampshire
President: Brant Elkind
Exec Director: Steven Wade
109 North State Street, Ste 2
Concord, NH 03301
Phone: 603-225-8400
In State: 800-773-8400
Fax: 603-228-6749
E-mail: mail@bianh.org
Website: www.bianh.org

BIA of New Jersey
President: Glenn McCreesh
Exec Director: Barbara Geiger-Parker
1090 King George Post Rd., Suite 708
Edison, NJ 08837
Phone: 732-738-1002
In State: 800-669-4323
Fax: 732-738-1132
E-mail: info@bianj.org
Website: www.bianj.org

BIA of New Mexico
Board President: Dr. Mark Pedrotty
Exec Director: Clara Holguin
121 Cardenas NE
Albuquerque, NM 87108
Phone: 505-292-7414
In State: 888-292-7415
Fax: 505-271-8983
E-mail: braininjurynm@msn.com
Website: www.braininjurynm.org

BIA of New York
President: Michael Kaplen, Esq.
Exec Director: Judy Avner
10 Colvin Avenue
Albany, NY 12206-1242
Phone: 518-459-7911
In State: 800-228-8201
Fax: 518-482-5285
E-mail: info@bianys.org
Website: www.bianys.org

BIA of North Carolina
President: Ana King
Exec Director: Sandra Farmer
PO Box 10912
Raleigh, NC 27605
Phone: 919-833-9634
In State: 800-377-1464
Fax: 919-833-5415
E-mail: Sandra.farmer@bianc.net
Website: www.bianc.net

BIA of Ohio
President: Jon Fishpaw
Exec Director: Suzanne Minnich
855 Grand View Avenue, suite 225
Columbus, OH 43215- 1123
Phone: 614-481-7100
Fax: 614-481-7103
In State: 866-644-6242 ("Ohio BIA")
E-mail: Help@Biaoh.org
Website: www.biaoh.org

BIA of Oklahoma
President: Tracy Grammer
PO Box 88
Hillsdale, OK 73743-0088
Phone: lines under repair
In State: lines under repair
Fax: lines under repair
E-mail: information@braininjuryoklahoma.org
Website: www.braininjuryoklahoma.org

BIA of Oregon
President: Wayne Eklund
Executive Director: Sherry Stock
2145 NW Overton Street
Portland, OR 97210
Phone: 503-413-7707
In State: 800-544-5243
Fax: 503-413-6849
E-mail: biaor@biaoregon.org
Website: www.biaoregon.org

BIA of Pennsylvania
President: Stewart Cohen
Program Manager: Monica J. Vaccaro, MS
Monica's phone: 215-718-5052
2400 Park Drive
Harrisburg, PA 17110
Phone: 717-657-3601
In State: 866-635-7097
E-mail: info@biapa.org
Website: www.biapa.org

BIA of Rhode Island
President: Paula O'Connor
Exec Director: Sharon Brinkworth
935 Park Avenue, Suite 8
Cranston, RI 02910-2743
Phone: 401-461-6599
Fax: 401-461-6561
E-mail: braininjuryctr@biaofri.org
Website: biaofri.org

BIA of South Carolina
President: Philip Clarkson
Exec. Director: Joyce Davis
800 Dutch Square Blvd. Suite B-225
Columbia, SC 29210
Mailing Address: P. O. Box 21523
Columbia, SC 29221-1523
Phone: 803-731-9823
Toll Free: 800-290-6461 (in-state)
Fax: 803-731-4804
E-mail: scbraininjury@bellsouth.net
Website: www.biausa.org/SC

BIA of Tennessee
President: Guynn Edwards
151 Athens Way, Suite 100
Nashville, TN 37228
Phone: 615-248-5878
Toll Free: 877-757-2428
Fax: 615-248-5879
E-mail: biaoftn@yahoo.com
Website: www.biaoftn.org

BIA of Texas
President: Eric Makowski
316 W 12th Street, Suite 405
Austin, TX 78701
Phone: 512-326-1212
In State: 800-392-0040
Fax: 512-478-3370
E-mail: info@biatx.org
Website: www.biatx.org

BIA of Utah
President: Teresa Such-Niebar
Exec Director: Ron Roskos
1800 S West Temple, Suite 203
Salt Lake City, UT 84115
Phone: 801-484-2240
In State: 800-281-8442
Fax: 801-484-5932
E-mail: biau@sisna.com
Website: www.biau.org

BIA of Vermont
President: Bob Luce
Executive Director: Trevor Squirrell
P O Box 226
Shelburne, VT 05482
Phone: 802-985-8440
Toll Free: 877-856-1772
E-mail: biavtinfo@adelphia.net
Website: www.biavt.org

BIA of Virginia
President: Stephen M. Smith
Exec Director: Anne McDonnell
1506 Willow Lawn Drive, Suite 112
Richmond, VA 23230
Phone: 804-355-5748
In State: 800-334-8443
Fax: 804-355-6381
E-mail: info@biav.net
Website: www.biav.net

BIA of Washington State
President: Richard Adler, Esq.
Exec Director: Gene van den Bosch, MA, MPA
3516 S. 47th Street, Suite 100
Tacoma, WA 98409
Phone: 253-238-6085
In State: 800-523-5438
Fax: 253-238-1042
E-mail: info@biawa.org
Website: www.biawa.org

BIA of West Virginia
President: Michael Davis
PO Box 574
Institute, WV 25112-0574
Phone: 304-766-4892
In State: 800-356-6443
Fax: 304-766-4940
E-mail: biawv@aol.com
Website: www.biausa.org/WVirginia

BIA of Wisconsin
President: Jeff Cameron
Director of Operations: Patricia David
N 35 W21100 Capitol Drive, Suite 5
Pewaukee, WI 53072
Phone: 262-790-9660
In State: 800-882-9282
Fax: 262-790-9670
E-mail: biaw@execpc.com
Website: www.biaw.org

BIA of Wyoming
President: Larry Plemmons
Exec Director: Dorothy Cronin
111 West 2nd Street, Suite 106
Casper, WY 82601
Phone: 307-473-1767
Nationwide: 800-643-6457
Fax: 307-237-5222
E-mail: biaw@tribcsp.com
Website: www.biausa.org/Wyoming

State Contacts

The following are Brain Injury Community contacts in their respective states. The Brain Injury Association of America lists these contacts for informational purposes only and does not review, support, endorse, or guarantee the information, services or activities of these organizations.

Alabama
Alabama Head Injury Foundation, Inc.
3100 Lorna Road, Suite 226
Hoover, Ala. 35216
Phone: (205) 823-3818
Fax: (205) 823-4544
E-Mail: charlespriest@bellsouth.net
Website: www.ahif.org

You may also contact the Brain Injury Association of America's National Family HelpLine at (800) 444-6443 or FamilyHelpline@biausa.org

Alaska
For any questions regarding service or assistance in Alaska, please contact The Brain Injury Association of America's National Family HelpLine at (800) 444-6443 or FamilyHelpline@biausa.org

The Traumatic Brain Injury Resource Directory (TBIRD)

You may also contact the Brain Injury Association of America's National Family HelpLine at (800) 444-6443 or FamilyHelpline@biausa.org

Louisiana
Brain Injury Alliance of Louisiana (BIALA)
P.O. Box 57527
New Orleans, LA 70157
Phone: 504-619-9989
Toll Free: 1-800-500-2026

For any questions regarding service or assistance in Louisiana, please contact The Brain Injury Association of America's National Family HelpLine at (800) 444-6443 or FamilyHelpline@biausa.org

Nebraska
For any questions regarding service or assistance in Nebraska, please contact The Brain Injury Association of America's National Family HelpLine at (800) 444-6443 or FamilyHelpline@biausa.org

Nevada
For any questions regarding service or assistance in Nevada, please contact The Brain Injury Association of America's National Family HelpLine at (800) 444-6443 or FamilyHelpline@biausa.org

North Dakota
Open Door Center
209 2nd Avenue, S.E.
Valley City, ND 58072
Phone: (701) 845-1124
Fax: (701) 845-1175

You may also contact the Brain Injury Association of America's National Family HelpLine at (800) 444-6443 or FamilyHelpline@biausa.org

South Dakota
South Dakota Brain Injury Alliance can be found online at:
www.braininjurysd.org
Please contact: Ron Hoops, President - (605) 395-6655 - e-mail:
rmmfarm@nrctv.com

For information about brain injury resources in South Dakota, You may also contact the Brain Injury Association of America's National Family HelpLine at (800) 444-6443 or FamilyHelpline@biausa.org